3 DAYS IN MILAN
Your local guide to Milan

www.3daysinmilan.com

Copyright © 2025 Blast21 Srl

Via Aosta 4A

20155 Milano

All rights reserved.

Cover image credits:
Katsiaryna Kashtalyan/shutterstock

TABLE OF CONTENTS

Table of Contents	3
Is Milan worth a trip?	**12**
How to get to Milan	**14**
Milan by plane	14
Transfers to Milan from the airport	14
Milan By car	16
Circulating in Milan by car	16
Parking on the street	17
Milan by train	17
Public transport in Milan	18
The tip: pay with your card	19
Public transport tickets	20
Taxis in Milan	22
Car Sharing and Bike Sharing	23
Where to sleep in Milan	**25**
Where and what to eat	**40**
Coperto and tipping	
Milanese cuisine restaurants	43
Luxury restaurants in Milan	44
Italian cuisine restaurants	46
Where to eat pizza	48
Where to have a snack	50
Non-Italian restaurants	51
Japanese restaurants in Milan	51
Chinese restaurants in Milan	52

    Indian restaurants in Milan   53
    Other international cuisines   53
Aperitif and dinner with a view   53
    Luxury Terrace restaurants   56
    Dinners and aperitifs on the terrace: cheaper options   57
    Where to buy a panettone?   58
    Where to eat a good ice cream   59
Where to go out at night in Milan   61

What to visit in Milan   **64**
    the History of Milan at a glance   64
    The must-sees: what to see in Milan in a day   71
    The unmissable works of art in Milan   74

Milan area by area: what to see   **82**
    The centre and the cathedral area   82
        The Duomo   82
        Piazza del Duomo   84
        Galleria Vittorio Emanuele   85
        The Museo del Novecento   86
        Piazza della Scala   87
        Gallerie d'Italia   88
        Leonardo Museum 3   89
        La Rinascente shopping mall   90
        Piazza dei Mercanti and surroundings   90
        Piazza degli Affari   91
        Velasca Tower   91
        The Pinacoteca Ambrosiana   92
        Walk from the Duomo to San Babila   93
        Brera district   94

The Brera Art Gallery	94
The Castello Sforzesco (Sforza Castle)	95
The Sforza Castle Museums	97
The Park Sempione	98
The Triennale (design and contemporary art museum)	99
The Arco della Pace	100
Piazzale Cadorna	102
Leonardo's Last Supper (Santa Maria delle Grazie)	102
San Maurizio al Monastero Maggiore (FREE!)	105
The Archaeological Museum (Museo archeologico)	106
Basilica Sant'Ambrogio (FREE)	107
Promenade along Via Torino	109
The South of Milan	110
The Basilica of San Lorenzo and the Columns	110
Church of Sant'Eustorgio	111
The Navigli	113
Church of St. Euphemia	114
Mudec - Museum of Cultures	115
The Prada Foundation (Fondazione Prada)	116
North East Milan: from Corso Venezia to Buenos Aires	116
Quadrilatero della Moda - Fashion District	116
Poldi Pezzoli Museum	117
A stroll along Corso Venezia	118
Etruscan Museum - Luigi Rovati Foundation	120
Natural History Museum	121
Porta Venezia	121
The Art Nouveau houses of Via Malpighi	121
A stroll along Corso Buenos Aires	121

    Boschi di Stefano House Museum   123

Milan North West   123
    Porta Nuova   123
    Corso Como   125
    The Isola District   125
    Via Paolo Sarpi - Chinatown   126
    The Monumental Cemetery (FREE)   127
    Corso Sempione   128
    City Life district   128
    San Siro Stadium   129
    The Certosa (Charterhouse) of Garegnano   130

Milan North   131
    Stazione Centrale - Central Station   131
    The Pirellone   132
    Palazzo Lombardia and its terrace   132
    Hangar Bicocca (FREE)   133

Milan... for enthusiasts   135
    If you love ancient history: Roman Milan   135
    If you love modern history: the 20th century in Milan   141
    If you love horror: the most macabre places in Milan   146
    If you love architecture: the Skyscraper Tour   151
    If you love football: Milan and Inter Tour   156
    If you love art: Leonardo da Vinci's Milan   164
    If you love art: discovering Hayez's Kisses   168

The tip: save money with tourist passes   173

Beyond Milan: 1-day TRIPS	179
Lake Como	179
Venice	179
Verona	180
Monza	180
Turin	181
Lake Maggiore	181
Cinque Terre	
Mantua	183
Bergamo Alta	183
Vigevano	184
Pavia	184
Special Occasions in Milan	186
Christmas and New Year in Milan	186
Milan Fashion Week	188
The Salone del Mobile and Design Week	191

Take Your Notes Here!

3 DAYS IN MILAN

How to read this guide

This guide was written by the 3daysinmilan.com website team. We want to provide visitors with a useful, handy book to discover our city.

We started our website with the idea of giving a personal point of view and advice, based on our tastes and experience.

You may end up in places where tourists usually don't go - and we may ignore activities that are popular on social media or mainstream, international travel guides.

In this guide, you simply find places we like and stuff we would suggest to friends visiting the city. By the way, all restaurants, hotels, activities you find in this guide are mentioned for free.

You will find some QR codes to scan and get access to some exclusive offers by our partner. For the sake of transparency, we want you to know that if you activate a service, or book a room, a guided tour, a transfer from a partner service, we will earn a commission from your purchase. These partnerships are marked as "SPONSORED TIP" and can be clearly identified.

Whenever possible, for each place we have indicated the address, closing times, possible ticket price, website, and other useful information for your visit.

When you find the abbreviation 'MM' followed by a number, we refer to the nearest metro station.

Each number indicates a different line:

- MM1 - Red
- MM2 - Green

- MM3 - Yellow
- MM4 - Blue
- MM5 - Lille

When we give you **directions**, we assume that you will use an app like Google Maps, Waze, or another navigator. If you are afraid of consuming too much data traffic, you can buy a virtual SIM valid for Italy with a service like Airalo.

In the list of attractions and restaurants, you will find some symbols to help you understand if they can interest you and how much they cost.
We use the Euro symbol, "€", to indicate if a hotel or a restaurant is expensive. The more Euros you see, the more expensive it is to dine or sleep there.

If something went wrong while visiting an attraction, eating in a restaurant or staying in a hotel; or if you found an error in this guide, please send a report to info@3giorniamilano.it.

SPONSORED TIP
Surf the web like a local: get a virtual SIM

Surf the internet freely during your holiday in Milan and in Italy. Don't be without internet: with Airalo you can buy a virtual SIM with gigabytes of internet traffic to use in Italy.

And top it up via the app, if and when you need to. Scan the QR Code and find the SIM for you.

Is Milan worth a trip?

Milan, after the 2015 Universal Exhibition, has become increasingly popular as a tourist destination. In 2023 there was a boom in tourists, with 8.5 million arrivals. On average, half a million tourists every month, with a peak of around 900,000 in July 2023.

The idea of Milan as a city for 'business only' travel is now gone and there is tourism all year round, even in summer.

Milan is a big city with a lot to offer to different types of visitors. In this guide, we will give good advice to those who are visiting Milan for the first time and want to get a 'taste' of it in two or three days. And also to those who have already been to the city and want to discover new sides.

There are indeed several reasons to visit Milan.

To art lovers, Milan offers a first-class artistic and cultural heritage, even if it is less evident than in other Italian cities: there is no shortage of artistic masterpieces from the Renaissance, for example, in the museums, but it is above all to enthusiasts of the 19th and 20th centuries that the city has much to offer.

It goes without saying that lovers of design and style will find many interesting things in Milan. The city is considered one of the fashion capitals of the world and offers unique opportunities both for shopping and for visiting museums and showrooms dedicated to design and style.

Gastronomy enthusiasts can take the opportunity to delve into the cuisine of Lombardy, little known abroad but, after all, also in the rest of Italy. Not to mention the range of ethnic cuisine available in the city.

There are also excellent restaurants in the city that explore international cuisine.

Sports enthusiasts can enjoy discovering the football teams A.C. Milan and F.C. Internazionale.

Milan is also an excellent starting point for day trips to various cities and tourist regions in central and northern Italy: Turin, Venice, Verona, and Bologna. But also Monza, Como, Lake Maggiore and Lake Orta, Bergamo, Brescia, Lake Iseo and Lake Garda, Alba and the wine-growing areas of Piedmont, Parma. All locations that can be reached quickly from Milan.

How to get to Milan

Milan by plane

Reaching Milan by plane is undoubtedly the most convenient solution, especially for those arriving from afar.

Milan is served by three main airports:

- Linate, a city airport connected to the city centre by a brand-new metro line, where many European airlines and even some low-cost flights land;
- Malpensa, used by intercontinental and long-haul flights, and therefore also by major airlines, is also the airport of choice for EasyJet (at Terminal 2) and with some flights also for Ryanair, Volotea etc.
- Orio al Serio, an airport in the city of Bergamo which, due to its proximity to Milan, has become a de facto choice for many airlines, especially Ryanair.

The main airlines connecting Milan to other Italian cities are ITA, Ryanair, Easyjet and Volotea.

Transfers to Milan from the airport

Linate is connected to the centre of Milan by the brand new M6 metro. The whole line is now fully operative and all the stations are open. The M4 takes you from

Linate to San Babila square, very close to the Duomo Cathedral, in less than 15 minutes.

From Malpensa or Bergamo airport you can reach the centre of Milan by bus and, only from Malpensa, by train.

At Milan Malpensa, you also have access to ShareNow car sharing, a service available in other European cities: if you are already a ShareNow user in Vienna, Amsterdam, Cologne, Hamburg, Berlin, Paris, Munich or Madrid, you can also use your app in Milan to rent cars, move around the city and get to the airport.

If you prefer comfort, you can take a taxi by following the signs at Arrivals. Or hire an airport transfer service.

SPONSORED TIP
Book a private transfer from the airport to the centre

If you land at Linate, the underground will take you to the centre of Milan in just 12 minutes. But if you arrive at Malpensa or Bergamo, you can expect at least an hour's journey by train or bus. Furthermore, there are no buses or trains late at night. Book a private transfer if you want to travel in peace after a long journey.

Milan By car

Milan is easily accessible by car thanks to many motorways.

There are many car parks on the outskirts of the city, at the metro terminals, which allow you to leave your car even for several days.

These include:

Bisceglie, northwest: 181 spaces, open until 1am. Daily cost €7.50, but there are extra charges for special events.

Romolo, south: 270 seats, open until 1am. Daily cost 7,50 euros, but there are extra rates in case of special events.

Rogoredo, south ext: 669 seats, open until 1am. Daily cost 7,50 euro, but there are extra rates in case of special events.

Cascina Gobba, north-east: 1,384 seats, open until 1am. Daily cost 7.50 euro, but there are extra charges for special events.

In these car parks, you can leave your car in the car park during closing times, but not collect it.

A good car park, close to the city centre, is **Vittor Pisani**, 943 spaces, 36.40 euro per day, open 24/7.

Circulating in Milan by car

Several restricted traffic zones are in force in Milan. We advise against using a car without the support of a navigator, even in the form of an app, which marks these zones.

The city centre falls under Area C, which requires payment of a permit to enter with a non-electric vehicle. The area is active from Monday to Friday, 7:30 am to 7:30 pm, but is expected to be extended to weekends in 2025.

PARKING ON THE STREET

Street-side parking spaces are delimited by coloured stripes. The yellow ones are reserved for residents, the blue ones require payment, the white ones (very rare) are free.

In the most central streets, you cannot park for more than two consecutive hours, not even for a fee.

MILAN BY TRAIN

Milan is connected to major Italian and European cities by high-speed or international trains. The main stations are Milano Centrale, Porta Garibaldi and Rogoredo. There is also the Rho Fiera station, useful for those who are in town for work.

Turin and Bologna can be reached in about 1 hour by Frecciarossa or Italo trains. Florence in 1 hour and 40 minutes, Rome in about 3 hours and Naples in just over 4 hours. Local trains and rail loops connect Milan to the suburbs and neighbouring towns.

Interregional, intercity and eurocity trains connect Milan to Venice in just 2 ½ hours, and Genoa in 1 ½ hours.

SPONSORED TRIP
Find your train on Omio

Milan is served by several railway operators. The former monopolist Trenitalia operates both local trains and intercity and very fast Frecciarossa trains. Trenord, which manages local trains, and Italo, which operates high-speed trains, are also Italian. Swiss, French, Austrian and German railways also arrive in Milan.

On Omio you can explore all the trains to Milan, as well as flights and buses!

PUBLIC TRANSPORT IN MILAN

Getting around Milan by public transport is very simple, fast, and intuitive, you can choose from various options ranging from the classic metro to Uber and car sharing services.

Getting around the city without having your own car is a very common choice among the Milanese and tourists: you don't have the stress of parking, no-go zones, petrol and fines, and you can be transported just about anywhere in comfort

The main means of public transport in Milan are the metro, tram and bus, which you can decide according to where you are starting from and where you want to go.

The metro has five lines and provides access to most parts of the city and the entire centre.

Scan this QR code to download the metro map:

Many tourists and visitors still choose to use trams, if only to experience them. Some lines, for example, such as the 1, are served by historic cars, certainly suggestive for those coming from a city, or an area, where trams are not served.

Buses serve the entire city, including the centre, but to avoid confusion with stops, it may be more convenient to use the metro. Remember that the city centre of Milan is relatively small and can be explored easily on foot.

THE TIP: PAY WITH YOUR CARD

Paying for public transport in Milan is particularly easy. As already happens in many European cities, instead of buying tickets you can use your contactless payment card, or a smartphone wallet such as Apple Pay, Android Pay, Samsung Pay, with NFC functionality.

To pay for public transport in Milan by card, simply place your card against the POS symbol found at the metro turnstiles, or on trams and buses. In the case of the metro, you must also put the same card down when you leave the metro.

<u>Please note: you cannot use the card on Trenitalia and Trenord trains, except for the Malpensa Express.</u>

Based on the number of journeys we make within 24 hours, the system will automatically charge the cheapest ticket for us.

Every 24 hours, the ticket management system calculates how many rides you have made and, based on those, finds the cheapest ticket for you and charges you for the amount needed. If you have taken two underground rides, for example, you will probably pay for two simple single rides. If, on the other hand, you have taken the metro several times in the course of the day, you will probably be charged for one day's ticket - quite a saving compared to paying for many single rides!

Public transport tickets

If you really don't want to use a payment card, or you don't have one for each passenger, you can buy different types of tickets that allow you to optimise your expenses and save a little, when possible.

ATM tickets can be bought at tobacconists in all Milan metro stations, at the many automatic machines in the stations, online via the Visit Milano app and the official ATM app called App ATM Milano.

ATM tickets allow you to travel on the ATM urban network and on the city sections of all interurban lines, on the Trenord urban network, including the Passante Ferroviario.

Each ticket is valid for a single access to the ATM urban network and must be validated at the entrance at the beginning of each journey and at each change of vehicle, respecting its time validity.

Since a few years now, validation must also be done at the exit, which is why you should always keep your ticket handy.

The transport fare system is based on concentric zones: the entire city of Milan is included in the Mi1 zone and requires a standard ticket. If you pay for your trip with a contactless card, the payment system will automatically calculate the fare for you.

If, on the other hand, you really want to buy a ticket and have to leave the urban area of Milan, a map of the fare zones can be found at this link:

https://nuovosistematariffario.atm.it/static/tariffe/stibm/zoom.png

City tickets cost EUR 2.20 and are used for travel on the urban network, allow one access to the metro and have a total duration of 90 minutes. For city tickets, you can take advantage of packages and promotions that allow you to save a little and are very useful for those who want to get around the city or have various business appointments.

Intercity tickets are used for travel on the interurban network, i.e. to travel from Milan to hinterland towns or between municipalities in the interurban area served by the metro. Fares change according to the destination to be reached, the various areas are divided into zones and single ticket prices range from 1.60 to 4.20 euro, validity ranges from 60 to 165 minutes.

In order not to risk, we advise you to use a contactless card.

If you are in Milan for business, and you need to go to RhoFiera Milano, for example to attend a congress, you must use a ticket for the Mi3 band, departing from the Mi1 band.

Even to go to the Forum di Assago you need a Mi3 band ticket. The San Siro Stadium, on the other hand, is in the Mi1 bracket.

Again: use your payment card, and forget about all that fuss.

Taxis in Milan

Milan has an extensive taxi network that covers every part of the city. In the centre, at airports and main stations, they are already parked and ready for rides, but can also be booked by phone or with an app.

The main Taxi Apps

- itTaxi
- Taxi App
- ShareNow
- Uber

Useful tip: these apps do not only work in Milan, but also in other Italian (and European, in the case of Share Now) cities. If you live in Italy, or travel there often, it can be useful to download them, register and add your payment card

Some apps allow you to pay with the credit or debit card you have saved on your phone, but you should always tell the taxi driver that you 'want to pay with the app' at the beginning of the ride, not at the end.

Most taxis in Milan accept credit card payments, and you can also use Tinaba and Alipay.

Instead, these are the main telephone numbers to call a taxi:

- Yellow Taxi 026969
- Blue Taxi 024040
- Radio Taxi 028585

CAR SHARING AND BIKE SHARING

Car sharing, scooter sharing and bike sharing services are convenient and versatile, allowing vehicles to be rented easily and quickly, even if only for a few hours or a short trip.

Sharing services are divided into two types: station-based services where bicycles or cars are picked up and delivered at dedicated, fixed stations, and free-floating services that allow vehicles to be reserved via an app and left parked on the street when the service is over.

As far as bicycles and e-bikes are concerned, the services of Lime and Dott, which are also present in many other cities around the world, are active. In most cases, these bicycles have to be parked within specific zones, which can be clearly identified on the map by the 'P' symbol in a blue circle.

There is a municipal Bike Sharing service, BikeMi, which provides parking at fixed stations in the area and requires a special registration.

As far as scooter sharing is concerned, however, at the moment the only international service that is still active is entrusted to Dott. The same rules apply as for bicycles: you have to park correctly, without disturbing traffic or pedestrians, and in the areas shown on the map with the 'p' symbol.

In car sharing there are two international services, ShareNow and Zity, and one Italian service, Enjoy. Car sharing cars can be parked on blue and yellow lines without paying anything. With these vehicles it is also possible to enter Area C without paying.

The respective apps show any areas where vehicles are not allowed to park, or there is a charge.

Where to sleep in Milan

Milan, one of the most fascinating cities in Italy, offers a wide range of neighbourhoods in which to stay. Whether you are in town for business, tourism or special events, finding the right area for your hotel can make all the difference.

In a nutshell

- The Center is ideal for those visiting Milan for the first time, with attractions such as the Duomo and the Castello Sforzesco.
- Brera is perfect for those seeking a romantic and artistic setting, with boutiques and art galleries.
- Navigli is the best area for those who love nightlife and are looking for a lively and dynamic stay.
- Porta Venezia is a lively and inclusive neighbourhood, ideal for the LGBTQ+ community and those who love art and culture.
- The Central Station is convenient for those arriving by train and offers easy connections to the rest of the city.

1. Historic Centre

In the area around Milan Cathedral there are many hotels of all categories, from luxury to budget. Unfortunately, as in all tourist cities, there is a risk of being fooled by online photographs and ending up in an overpriced room.

So here is our list of the best hotels in central Milan, with different choices based on your budget, selected according to the personal experience of travellers.

€€€€ - Super luxury

Hotel Mandarin Oriental Milan, via Andegari 9, MM1 MM3 Duomo

In the heart of the fashion capital, the Mandarin Oriental Milan is a perfect example of Italian design combined with oriental tradition. Located in four prestigious 18th-century buildings, the hotel is just a short walk from La Scala and offers 104 extraordinarily elegant rooms and suites. The 72 rooms are refined and characterized by a well-studied layout of the spaces and a neutral color palette. The 32 suites, including the Presidential Suite, are spacious and luxurious. It includes a spa with wellness centre, an indoor pool and a gym.

Park Hyatt Milano, via Tommaso Grossi 1, MM1 MM3 Duomo

Located opposite the entrance to the Galleria Vittorio Emanuele, in the heart of the fashion district, the Park Hyatt Milan is just 200 meters from Milan Cathedral and the Teatro alla Scala.

In addition to its perfect location, the hotel offers a spa, restaurant and bar, and well-kept rooms, some of which have an exclusive view of the city center.

Hotel Viu Milan, via A. Fioravanti 6, MM5 Monumentale MM2 MM5 Porta Garibaldi

A hotel in the Porta Garibaldi station district, it is a new building, with clean architecture and high quality materials. It offers a spa and a fully equipped gym. A distinctive feature is the swimming pool on the top floor of the building, with a 360 degree view of the city. There is also a rooftop bar for aperitifs.

€€€ - Expensive

Hotel Straf, via San Raffaele 3 MM3 Duomo

In one of the side streets next to the Duomo, right in the center. A hotel with a very modern, brutalist design, with metal elements. Designer rooms, high level service.

Hotel Gran Duca di York, via Moneta 1, MM3 Duomo MM2 Cordusio

Right in the center, near the Pinacoteca Ambrosiana, this small hotel offers a personalized service. The price is commensurate with the quality and the super central location.

€€ - Cheap but comfortable

Hotel Ariston, Largo del Carrobbio 2 MM3 Missori

Close to the Duomo, you can reach everything on foot. An anonymous building, beautiful interiors.

Hotel Fenice, Corso Buenos Aires 2 MM1 Porta Venezia

A hotel with a few dozen rooms, overlooking one of the busiest streets in the city, a stone's throw from the LGBTQ+ district and about ten minutes' walk from San Babila and the Duomo. Some rooms face the interior and are quieter.

Eurohotel, Via Sirtori 24, MM1 Porta Venezia

In a quiet side street, but still close to everything. The hotel has a main building and several annexes. It also has a small room equipped for training, a swimming pool and a spa.

€ - Hostels

Ostello Bello, via Medici 4 MM3 Missori

A few steps from the Duomo, well-connected by subway, within walking distance of the main monuments and tourist areas, including the Navigli. It offers both dormitories and private rooms with bathroom. It also offers a shared kitchen, a common room, and vending machines that are always open.

2. Brera

Brera is one of Milan's most exclusive districts, located north of the Duomo. This district is famous for the Pinacoteca di Brera, an art gallery housing medieval and Renaissance works, especially from northern Italy. Strolling through Brera, one can discover small cafés, original shops and green corners that give the neighbourhood a unique atmosphere.

Brera is also known for its restaurants, clubs and art galleries, making it a lively and dynamic area. However, accommodation prices here are quite high, reflecting the exclusivity of the district. If you are looking for a luxurious and comfortable stay, Brera is definitely one of the best options in Milan.

So far, we have no suggestions in this district. But we are working on that!

3. Navigli

Staying in a hotel in the Navigli area of Milan is a choice made by many tourists. It is certainly the most lively and vibrant district in the city, especially in the evening, with many options for an aperitif, dinner or after-dinner drinks.

With a walk or by public transport, you can reach the Duomo and the main attractions of the city in about ten minutes.

There are many hotels in the Navigli district, we have selected some of the best for you, with different options for all budgets

€€€€ - Luxury

Maison Borella, alzaia Naviglio Grande 8, MM2 Porta Genova

Hotel on the Naviglio Grande in a modern building. It also offers an in-house restaurant.

€€ - Cheap but quality hotels

Art Hotel Navigli, via Fumagalli 4, MM2 Porta Genova

A modern hotel with a good level of comfort in the rooms. Restaurants, bars, and nightlife are within easy walking distance.

Hotel Milano Navigli, piazza Sant'Eustorgio 3, MM2 Porta Genova

A modern and efficient hotel, in a beautiful square in the centre of Milan. The nightlife of the Navigli is very close by, but the Duomo is also just a few minutes' walk away.

€ - Hostels

Combo, 83 ripa di Porta Ticinese, MM2 Porta Genova

A hostel on the canals with a total of 200 beds in dormitories and private rooms. It is located in the Navigli district, ideal for those who want to go out in the evening and stay out late. There is also a shared kitchen available for travellers.

4. Porta Venezia

Porta Venezia is one of Milan's most charming districts, suitable for everyone, from families to young people to the LGBTQ+ community, that gathers around via Lecco at night. The area is well served by public transport, with the underground stations of Palestro and Porta Venezia (M1).

Moreover, the proximity to the Central Station makes it easy to travel by train for excursions in the surrounding area.

Lately, however, the area is not always safe in the late night.

€€ - Cheap but good quality hotels

Hotel Due Giardini, 47 Via Benedetto Marcello, MM3/MM2 Centrale – MM1 Lima

A small, simple hotel between the Central Station and Corso Buenos Aires. Nothing exceptional, but clean and good value for money. Don't be put in the annex, stay in the main building.

Hotel Stradivari, via Stradivari 4, MM2/MM1 Loreto

A hotel on the second floor of an unremarkable building. Good value for money, it's best to ask for a room facing the interior because the area can be noisy.

5. Isola

Isola is a district of Milan that has undergone a major transformation in recent years, becoming a lively and dynamic area. Located between Stazione Centrale and Stazione Porta Garibaldi, it is well-connected thanks to several metro stations such as Isola MM5, Gioia MM2 and Garibaldi FS MM2/MM5, as well as numerous bus and tram lines.

This district is famous for its modernity and its skyscrapers, including the Bosco Verticale and the UniCredit headquarters building, the tallest in Italy. If you love modern atmospheres and skyscrapers, Isola is the right place for you.

6. Sempione

The area around Parco Sempione is one of the most popular with fashionistas. Here you are close to the centre, but also to the new trendy area of Milan called CityLife. It is the perfect place for those who love trendy restaurants and bars. You can find many places to have an aperitif and drink excellent cocktails, but also elegant restaurants where you can enjoy refined dishes from all over the world.

The closest underground stations are Domodossola MM5, Gerusalemme MM5, Tre Torri MM5. Corso Sempione itself is well served by trams.

The Parco Sempione district is considered the green lung of the city due to its many green areas. The area is also home to important attractions such as the Castello Sforzesco, the aquarium and the Palazzo dell'Arte. A quiet area, well served by public transport and full of restaurants, Parco Sempione is ideal for those travelling with families or children.

€€€ - Medium-high range

Hotel Lancaster, via A. Sangiorgio 16, MM5 Domodossola

A mid-range hotel in an Art Nouveau building, a good choice if you don't want to spend too much but still want to be comfortable. The area offers many options for breakfast, lunch and dinner. The CityLife district and Corso Sempione are within walking distance. The metro and trams guarantee a quick connection to the city centre.

€€ - Cheap but good quality hotels

Hotel Losanna, 39 Via Piero della Francesca, MM5 Gerusalemme

A hotel with about 20 rooms of a good standard, well connected by the underground in a neighbourhood with lots of restaurants, cafes and bars. The centre can be reached on foot or by underground and tram (lines 12, 14, 1 and 19 in the vicinity). The reception staff can also explain which buses to take to reach the centre.

€ - Hostels

Meininger, via privata Giovanni Calvino 11, MM5 Cenisio

A hostel with excellent value for money, in a neighbourhood full of restaurants and a short walk from the MM5 underground station and tram lines 12 and 14, which will take you to the Duomo in about 10-15 minutes.

7. San Siro

If you're in Milan to see a football match or a concert, you're probably looking for a hotel near San Siro, the Milan stadium.

It's an understandable choice. During major events at the stadium, in fact, metro stations are often closed for security reasons, road traffic is interrupted, and the crowd is asked to disperse on foot.

This creates a certain amount of confusion, and it can take a long time to find public transport, a taxi or to get out of the traffic jam in your car.

€€€€ - Luxury

Sheraton Milan San Siro, Via Caldera 3, 2 km from the stadium

High-level structure with all comforts a couple of kilometres from the stadium.

Melià Milano, via Masaccio 19, MM1 MM5 Lotto

Historic luxury hotel in the Lotto area, 1.3 kilometres from the Stadium, about 20 minutes on foot.

€€€ - Medium-High Range

B&B Hotel Milano San Siro, via Achille 4, MM5 San Siro

A few steps from the San Siro Stadium, this hotel of the successful 'B&B' hotel chain offers functional rooms, in line with the chain's standard, in a perfect location for those who want to attend an event at the stadium.

Residence Portello Milano, via Mosè Bianchi 75, MM1 Amendola MM4 Segesta

This establishment offers flats, furnished in a residential style and is located 1.5 km from San Siro and about 500 metres from Leonardo da Vinci's Last Supper. It is therefore very functional accommodation for those who are in Milan to follow an event at the stadium but also want to take the opportunity to visit the city centre.

€€ - Cheap but good quality

Le Querce Hotel, via Jacopo della Quercia 6, MM1 MM4 Lotto

Simple, 2-star hotel, clean and basic, excellent location.

8. Central Station (Stazione Centrale) - Porta Garibaldi

The Milano Centrale and Milano Porta Garibaldi stations are located near the city centre and are very well-connected by train, underground and public transport.

€€€€ - Luxury

Hotel Excelsior Gallia Piazza Duca d'Aosta 9 MM2 MM3 Centrale

Hotel Excelsior Gallia is a recently renovated luxury classic in Milan. It is located opposite the Central Station. It has 235 rooms, including 50 suites. It has a spa, a panoramic indoor pool and a fully equipped fitness area on the seventh floor. It has two snack bars, one on the ground floor and the other on the rooftop terrace, for aperitifs, after-dinner drinks or lunch. There is also a restaurant and a wine cellar for wine tasting.

Westin Palace, Piazza della Repubblica 20, MM3 Repubblica

An elegant and luxurious hotel with a modern façade and refined interiors. Spacious and comfortable rooms. The hotel offers restaurants and bars, a fitness centre and a wellness centre.

Principe di Savoia, Piazza della Repubblica 17, MM3 Repubblica

The Hotel Principe di Savoia is a historic five-star hotel located in the heart of Milan. It has a neoclassical façade and offers high-quality rooms and suites. The hotel restaurant is excellent, as is the bar service. It has a swimming pool and a wellness area.

Hotel Me il Duca, Piazza della Repubblica 13, MM3 Repubblica

A stylish hotel that opened a few years ago with a modern and sophisticated design. Rooms and suites are furnished in the same very modern style. Restaurant and bar, one of which is on the rooftop with a panoramic view of the city. It also offers a wellness area.

€€€ - Medium-high range

Starhotel Echo, viale Andrea Doria 4, MM2/MM3 Centrale

Next to the Central Station, this hotel offers an excellent location and beautiful rooms. The bar and restaurant are also very good.

NYX Milan Hotel, Piazza IV Novembre, MM2/MM3 Centrale

Very popular with tourists, this hotel is literally a stone's throw from the Central Station and is a giant of Milanese tourism. Over 300 rooms on 11 floors: a city in itself!

€€ - Cheap, but good quality

Hotel Due Giardini, 47 Via Benedetto Marcello, MM3/MM2 Centrale – MM1 Lima

A small, simple hotel between the Central Station and Corso Buenos Aires. Nothing exceptional, but clean and good value for money. Don't be put in the annex, stay in the main building.

€ - Hostels

Ostello Bello Grande, via R. Lepetit MM2/MM3 Centrale

Another hostel in the 'Ostello Bello' chain. It has both dormitories and single rooms. Reliable, clean, a safe bet for those who like hostels. With a nice extra: a roof terrace.

9. Porta Romana

The Porta Romana neighbourhood is located south-east of the centre of Milan and is a good choice for those looking for a hotel that is close to attractions and restaurants, but in a quiet area, and within easy reach of the centre.

€€€ - Average Price

BB Hotels – Aparthotel Bocconi, via P. Teulié 7, MM3 Porta Romana

A small apartment-hotel in a quiet area.

€€ - Budget

Hotel Five, corso Lodi 4, MM3 Porta Romana

A good solution for those who want to be close to the centre without spending too much.

€ - Hostels

Yellow Square Milan, via Servilliano Lattuada 14, MM3 Porta Romana

The Milanese branch of a chain of hostels, it has both dormitories and private rooms of excellent quality. It also offers a shared kitchen, some bars, a recreation area and several services. The Duomo can be reached by underground in 10-15 minutes.

Madama Hostel, via Benaco 1, MM3 Lodi

It stands out for its unique and lively atmosphere. Located in a historic building, it offers brightly coloured rooms and a bistro where you can eat.

10. Other Areas

If you want a room in Milan while saving a little money, the advice is to look a few metro stops away from the Duomo. **Corso Buenos Aires** is certainly well-connected and offers a lot of choice as far as hotels are concerned.

The area around the **Pagano** stop of the MM1 is also a good compromise: a residential neighbourhood but full of shops, restaurants, and bars.

If you want to spend less, you can try the 'business' hotels around **Viale Monza** (many MM1 stations, from Pasteur MM1 to Rovereto MM1 and up to Sesto Marelli MM1), in the Fiera area (MM5 **Portello**) and at the **Ca'Granda** stop on the MM5 line: you will be further away from the centre, but there are often interesting offers at weekends because these hotels are mainly used for business trips.

OTHER HOSTELS

Milan is a vibrant and cosmopolitan city, but it can be expensive. However, there are several cheap hostel options in the centre that offer comfort and sociability without emptying your wallet.

We mentioned some hostels in the previous pages, among other accommodation options in the most popular areas of the city.

Here are some others.

New Generation Hostel Milan Center Navigli, via Marco Burigozzo 11, Navigli

A great place if you love nightlife and culture. Located close to the canals, it offers a lively and dynamic environment. In the evenings, the Navigli comes alive with bars and restaurants, making this hostel ideal for young travellers.

Atmos Luxe Hostel, via Privata Paolo Cezanne, Navigli

It offers a relaxing yet fun environment. Located in a quiet area, it is ideal for those who want to enjoy some relaxation after a day of exploring. The rooms are cosy and well maintained, ensuring a pleasant stay.

Babila Hostel & Bistro, via Conservatorio 21, MM1 San Babila

An excellent choice if you seek a stylish and comfortable environment. Centrally located, this hostel offers modern and well-appointed rooms. It also has a bistro where you can enjoy delicious dishes without having to go out.

Hostel Aig Piero Rotta, via Martino Bassi 2, out of the centre

The Hostel Aig Piero Rotta combines tradition and modernity in a cosy atmosphere. The rooms are spacious and equipped with all the necessary amenities for a pleasant stay. The location is ideal for those wishing to explore both the city centre and the surrounding green areas.

What to eat in Milan

A very common joke in Italy says that 'the typical dish of Milan is sushi'. In reality, Milan and Lombardy have a solid culinary tradition, mainly made up of dishes that originate from a poor cuisine and readily available foodstuffs, even during the war.

The truth is that Milan has been welcoming immigrants from all over Italy and the world for decades. And as in all cosmopolitan cities of the world, everyone has brought their own traditions with them. So in Milan you can find excellent restaurants from every Italian region and from many countries. And yes, a lot of sushi, often Chinese-run: but that is a trend you can find in almost all of Europe.

If you are used to Italy's cuisines "outside of Italy", you will be quite surprised by the traditional dishes here in the norther region of Lombardy. According to tradition, pasta is often replaced by rice, butter is more present than elsewhere (although extra virgin olive oil now prevails, also for health and dietary reasons!), and polenta plays an important role.

Let's see what the typical Milanese dishes are and where to eat them.

Cotoletta alla milanese is a slice of suckling veal loin, first dipped in beaten egg and then in breadcrumbs, trying to get the breadcrumbs to stick. The real "cotoletta alla milanese" is strictly on the bone, cooked in a pan and fried in clarified butter.

It can also be found in the "vestita" (literally "dressed") version. The precious cutlet is garnished (hence "dressed") on top, typically with rocket, cherry tomatoes, and Parmesan cheese.

Purists will tell you that the "cotoletta" must be veal, cooked in butter and "not dressed", but the advice is to try it and make your own opinion.

Be careful when you order a cotoletta. In many restaurants you can find variants made with pork (you recognise it because the bone is shorter and rounder), chicken (absolutely unacceptable), and adult beef (here the difference is less recognisable).

In the next pages, you will find some good restaurants where you can have a real cotoletta.

Risotto alla Milanese is another iconic dish of the city. A first course that, according to tradition, was created by a painter who wanted to surprise his guests by colouring the rice with saffron, a spice he used for his paintings.

The traditional recipe includes a veal marrowbone, butter, saffron, and Parmesan cheese.

Veal ossobuco (shin steak) is a dish that appeared in Milanese cookery books as early as the 18th century. And it is often served on a 'bed' of saffron "risotto alla milanese". A perfect match. At the end of a long and slow cooking, our shin steak is decorated with 'gremolada', a minced garlic, lemon zest and parsley.

Cassoeula is a traditional dish from Lombardy, made with pork scraps, those that the nobility did not eat in the past. Therefore, in a cassoeula we find ribs, pork rinds, pig's foot, ears, and pig's tail, to which are added verzini (typical small pork sausages) and lots of cabbage. The poor origin of the dish required the use of cabbage frozen from the cold of winter, which could not be served to the rich bourgeoisie but was used by the poor people.

Among the typical Milanese dishes at risk of extinction are **gnervitt** ('nervetti' in Italian), which are the tendons of the calf's knee or shin, cooked in water for two hours and then cleaned and dressed with onion and pickles.

Mondeghili, on the other hand, are meatballs made from leftover meat, especially from roast and boiled meat. The meat is minced and mixed with sausage, mortadella, grated grana cheese and stale bread soaked in milk. Meatballs are formed and then fried in butter.

Rustin negàa are veal knots (on the bone) dipped in flour and cooked in a pan with butter, diced bacon and a sprig of rosemary. Everything is doused with white wine, covered with broth and then left to evaporate, then baked in the oven at 160 °C for an hour and a half.

WHERE TO EAT IN MILAN

COPERTO AND TIPPING

Understanding the "coperto"

On Italian restaurant menus and bills, you'll almost always find the item "coperto" (cover charge).

It's not a scam or a rip-off. The "cover charge" is perfectly legal and is always applied, even to Italian customers. It's a fixed cost that covers the expenses for tablecloths, plates, cutlery, bread, and service.

In more exclusive restaurants, on the other hand, you may find the item 'service', which is often in addition to the 'cover charge'.

Do I have to leave a tip?

Tipping is not part of Italian culture. Italians don't tip. For the service provided by the waiting staff, in fact, we already pay the 'cover charge'.

MILANESE CUISINE RESTAURANTS

We have already warned you. Tourist traps are a danger all over Italy, and Milan is not an exception. Especially when it comes to food.

Most restaurants say they offer Milanese dishes. But there is a risk of finding improvised dishes, such as chicken or a pork schnitzel, passed off as a "real cotoletta".

So here are some of our favourite places to eat Milanese: if you have other restaurants to suggest, write to us. We'll try them.

Trattoria Arlati €€€
Via Alberto Nota, 47 Reservations: thefork.it
Telephone: 02 643 3327

Restaurant in the northern area, very popular. Milanese and non-Milanese dishes, extensive wine list, average prices.

L'Altra Isola €€
Via Edoardo Porro, 8 Telephone: 02 6083 0205

Old-fashioned restaurant, informal service and real Milanese cuisine. Not far from the Isola, even on foot. Telephone reservations must be made well in advance.

Testina €€€
Via Abbadesse 19 Reservations: thefork.it wheno.it Telephone: 02 4035907

This restaurant in the northern part of the city offers a simple menu with some Milanese specialities. The wine list is extensive and includes Lombard labels that are not easy to find.

Al Garghet €€€
Via Selvanesco, 36 Telephone: 02 534698

Just outside Milan, nestled in the meadows, a very atmospheric restaurant, although already discovered by tourists of all nationalities. Schnitzel and more. It is essential to book well in advance.

€€€€ - LUXURY RESTAURANTS IN MILAN

Leading guides identify some important luxury restaurants in Milan. The Michelin Guide 2025, for example, envisages 16 starred restaurants in the city: 12 with 1 star, 3 with 2 stars and 1 restaurant with 3 stars.

Enrico Bartolini at Mudec, at the Museo delle Culture (Via Tortona 56)

3 DAYS IN MILAN

The only 3-star restaurant in Milan offers cuisine revisited in a contemporary key, with a strong innovation, proposed in an elegant setting and with a high level of service. Telephone number for reservations: 02 8429 3701 Email: info@enricobartolini.net - ristorante@enricobartolini.net

Here is a list of other luxury restaurants in Milan, all of them are to be considered "€€€€".

Andrea Aprea, Corso Venezia 52 (Fondazione Luigi Rovati), telephone number +39 02 38273030, email address info@andreaaprea.com

Verso Capitaneo, Piazza Duomo 21, telephone number +39 02 8975 0929

Seta by Antonio Guida, at the Mandarin Oriental hotel, Via Monte di Pietà, 18, phone number +39 02 8731 8897, email address momln-setarestaurant@mohg.com

Aalto Cucina by Takeshi Iwai, Alvar Aalto Square, telephone number +39 02 250 62 888, email address for reservations booking@aalto-restaurant.com

Anima, via Rosales 4, at Hotel Una Milano Verticale, telephone number +39 02.622.78.500, email address prenotazioni@ristoranteanima.com

Berton, 13 Mike Bongiorno Street, telephone number 02 67075801, email address info@ristoranteberton.com

Contraste, via Giuseppe Meda 2, phone number +39 02 49536597, email address info@contrastemilano.it

Il luogo di Aimo e Nadia, Via Privata Raimondo Montecuccoli, 6. Phone number. +39 02 416886, email. info@aimoenadia.com

ITALIAN CUISINE RESTAURANTS

€€€ Il Cormorano Sempione, Via Angelo Poliziano 1 – MM5 Gerusalemme or MM5 Domodossola — +39 94383205, online booking available

Seafood restaurant, elegant and fairly formal setting.

€€€ Il Cormorano Isola, Via L.P. Lambertenghi 34 – MM5 Isola — +39 02 69004384, online booking available

Seafood restaurant, cosy and informal atmosphere.

€€€ Zio Pesce Navigli, Via Cicco Simonetta 8 – MM4 De Amicis or MM2 Sant'Agostino

Online booking available, closed on Sundays Informal fish restaurant. An appetizer and a first course around 32/35 euros.

€ Pasta Fresca da Giovanni, Via Ascanio Sforza 31 – Navigli area

Informal environment, few seats. Fresh pasta to take away or eat in for a quick meal. Open for lunch; open for dinner on Friday, Saturday, and Sunday until 21.00. Closed on Tuesdays.

€€ Osteria Naviglio Grande, via Ludovico il Moro 139, Navigli area, online booking available

Italian restaurant serving meat and fish in the Navigli area. Informal setting. Good wine list with affordable local options.

€€ Osteria della Darsena, Via Vigevano 1, Navigli area, online booking on their website

Italian cuisine, with a prevalence of meat and some fish dishes. Informal environment.

€€€ Bauscia Brera, via dell'Orso 2, Duomo area, online booking on TheFork or Quandoo, closed on Sunday evenings.

Quite formal environment, Italian cuisine mainly with meat and several typical Lombard and Milanese dishes. 5 euros "coperto", cover charge. Interesting wine list with options for everyone.

€€ Locanda Perbellini Bistrot, via della Moscova 25, MM2 Moscova, online booking with Plateform or on their website. Open for lunch and dinner, closed on Sunday and Monday.

Restaurant with an elegant atmosphere, concise menu with traditional Italian dishes, some with a modern twist.

€€€ Trattoria Masuelli San Marco, viale Umbria 80, Porta Romana MM3 Lodi, +39 02 5518 4138

€€ Giannino l'Angolo d'Abruzzo, via Rosolino Pilo 20, Porta Venezia MM1

This successful restaurant serving Abruzzo cuisine has now opened several branches in various districts of Milan: you can look them up on Google. Here we give you the address of the first restaurant that opened, which serves typical cuisine from Abruzzo, a region in central Italy, with a prevalence of meat specialities.

€€€ La Brisa, via Francesco Ferrucci 1, MM5 Domossola

In the Sempione neighbourhood, an elegant restaurant specialising in Trentino Alto Adige, an Alpine region in north-eastern Italy. It offers dishes that are very rarely found outside Italy. And that are not easy to find even outside the region. Elegant but not formal atmosphere, excellent service, good wine list.

WHERE TO EAT PIZZA

There are several Neapolitan pizzeria chains in Milan. These are successful brands that have opened several restaurants in different neighbourhoods. Here are some of our favourites. Some, in addition to pizza, also have pasta, meat, or fish dishes on the menu.

€€ Pizzium Pizzerie

Dozens of restaurants in Italy, with the possibility to book online. In Milan these restaurants are in tourist areas, you can find others using Google Maps:

- via Arco, between Brera and the Sforzesco Castle, a stone's throw from the Duomo;
- via Buonarroti, near CityLife;
- via Pola, in the Isola district;
- via Procaccini, in the Sempione area;
- via Solari and via Vigevano, in the Navigli area;
- viale Doria, near the Central Station;
- viale Tunisia, near Porta Venezia.

€€ Quartieri Spagnoli

We recommend these two pizzerias, in the Cenisio MM5 and Sempione MM5 Gerusalemme areas, for a full immersion in the culture of Naples. Firstly thanks to the pizzas and the extensive menu ranging from appetisers to desserts. But above all with a very decorated environment and Neapolitan music in the background.

€€ Assaje

A chain of 'gourmet pizzerias' with many locations in Italy.

They are present in these tourist areas of Milan:

- via Casale 5, Navigli area;
- two restaurants, in via Pietro Borsieri 24 and via Traù 2, in the Isola area;

Largo La Foppa, between Moscova and Brera.

€€ Casa Sorbillo

The network of pizza chef Gino Sorbillo includes three restaurants in Milan. Casa Sorbillo Duomo (via Agnello 18), Casa Sorbillo San Babila (Largo Corsia dei Servi 11) and Casa Sorbillo Garibaldi (Piazza XXV Aprile 12, a stone's throw from Moscova and Piazza Gae Aulenti).

In Via Ugo Foscolo 1, practically in Galleria Vittorio Emanuele, a stone's throw from the Duomo, there is Gino Sorbillo Pizza Gourmand, a 'gourmet' version in the very centre of the city.

€ Spontini

A chain of 'pizza alta al taglio' (thick pizza by the slice) that was born and raised in Milan. It then became a franchise in Italy and abroad. If you search on Google Maps, you can easily find Spontini pizzerias in the Duomo, Brera, Navigli, Sempione, CityLife, Central Station, Porta Romana and Corso Buenos Aires areas.

€€€€ Crazy Pizza Milano, via Varese 2, online booking available on their website

The Milanese branch of Crazy Pizza has opened in the Moscova area. Crazy Pizza is a chain of 'gourmet pizzerias' with a touch of luxury. The pizzas are not cheap, not even the classic ones, but the menu includes some very special dishes, such as truffle pizza. The menu includes appetisers, first courses, main courses and desserts. It's not cheap but it's certainly an experience.

WHERE TO HAVE A SNACK

€ Luini Panzerotti, via Santa Radegonda 16, closed on Sundays, open from 10am to 8pm, <u>TAKE-AWAY ONLY</u>

In this historical place in Milan there is always a long line of locals and tourists. Luini has been baking its panzerotti since 1888: they are available fried, baked or sweet. Luini also sells other sweet and savoury products: given the long wait in the queue, it may be worth taking a few samples.

€€ Mercato Centrale Milano, access from the Central Station and via Sammartini, open every day from 7am to midnight

A food court-style gastronomic space that opened a few years ago: you can order from different shops and eat in a shared area with lots of tables and chairs.

You can find a bit of everything, to eat in or take away. Bread, coffee, desserts, meat, cheese, cold cuts, wine, fresh pasta, fish, beer, rice, truffles... even Chinese ravioli and sushi.

Non-Italian restaurants

Italian cuisine is famous and appreciated all over the world, but it can become tiresome, especially if you stay in the country for a long time. Milan is home to cuisines from many countries, in many cases with a quality recognised by the main international guides. Here is a selection of restaurants to try.

Japanese restaurants in Milan

€€€€ Iyo Taste Experience, via Piero della Francesca 74. Phone +39 02 454 76 898, email address info@iyo.it

The first Japanese restaurant in Milan to be awarded a Michelin star. Definitely a chic environment, reservations are essential, prices are high as is the quality.

€€€ Shiro Poporoya, via Bartolomeo Eustachi 20, Porta Venezia area, online booking available

One of the few Japanese restaurants in Milan that is 100% Japanese-run.

In the city there are also hundreds of Japanese restaurants, run by Chinese, that operate on the all you can eat formula. A variable fixed price, generally around 15 euros for lunch and between 23 and 30 for dinner, which does not include drinks, dessert, and cover charge.

CHINESE RESTAURANTS IN MILAN

€€€ Bon Wei, via Ludovico Castelvetro 16, MM5 Gerusalemme

This restaurant defines itself as 'high regional Chinese cuisine'. Very extensive menu of Chinese specialities with many refined ingredients.

€€ Wang Jiao, several restaurants in different areas of the city

Small chain of Chinese restaurants. Extensive menu, well-prepared dishes, informal service and good quality. Very busy, especially at the weekend, so it's advisable to book.

€ Jubin, via Paolo Sarpi 11

In the heart of Chinatown, one of Milan's historic Chinese restaurants.

€ Trattoria Long Chang, via Paolo Sarpi 42

Simple Chinese restaurant, genuine cuisine at affordable prices. Generous portions. Informal service, sometimes a little chaotic. Long waits at the weekend.

Indian restaurants in Milan

€€/€€€ Serendib, via Pontida 2, MM2 Moscova

Excellent Sri Lankan cuisine in this historic restaurant, very well known and popular in the city. Reservations recommended.

€€ Just India, via Benedetto Marcello 34, MM1 Lima / MM3 MM2 Centrale

This restaurant is run by Indians and frequented by many Indians living in the city. The food is traditional, wholesome, and inexpensive.

Other international cuisines

€€ Dawali, Via Corrado II il Salico 11, MM3 Lodi

Not very close to the metro, this Lebanese restaurant has excellent reviews on social media.

€€€ Bem Brasil, via Bessarione 5, MM3 Lodi

This Brazilian restaurant is a favourite with tourists and Milanese alike, at least judging by the reviews on TripAdvisor and Google.

APERITIF AND DINNER WITH A VIEW

Milan is a city that knows how to amaze, and its terraces with breathtaking views are the perfect place to do so. Imagine sipping a cocktail while admiring the unique skyline of this metropolis, a mix of modern architecture and historical monuments.

Each terrace offers a unique experience, combining delicious drinks with spectacular views. And many also allow dining.

€€€ Terrazza Aperol

Galleria Vittorio Emanuele II. MM3/MM1 Duomo. Open Monday to Sunday, 11am to 11pm, Saturday closing time postponed to 01:00am

Located in Piazza Duomo, Terrazza Aperol is the ideal place to feel at the heart of the city. With a spectacular view of the Duomo, it is perfect for an aperitif with friends or a break after a day of shopping. The atmosphere is lively and the cocktails are some of the best in town.

It does not accept reservations: you have to go there and stand in line.

€€€€ Ceresio 7

Via Ceresio 7. MM5 Monumentale or MM5/MM2 Porta Garibaldi. Open every day. Bar from 12:30 am to 1 am. Restaurant 12:30 am - 3 pm and 7:30 pm - 11 pm.

Ceresio 7 offers a luxurious experience with its two swimming pools and a panoramic view encompassing the whole of Milan. This rooftop is the ideal place for those seeking elegance and relaxation. The cocktails are carefully prepared and the ambience is refined, perfect for a special evening.

Only the restaurant can be booked online, not the bar.

€€€ Radio Rooftop Bar
Via Marco Polo 18. MM3 Repubblica. Daily from 7am to midnight.

If you are looking for a cosmopolitan atmosphere, the Radio Rooftop Bar is the place to be. Located on the top floor of the ME Milan Il Duca, it offers a 360-degree view of the city.

Here you can enjoy an aperitif or an after-dinner drink in a chic, modern ambience with an international touch that makes the experience unique.

€€€ The Roof
Via Alberico Albricci 2. MM3 Missori. Open from 12 to 01am (02 Fridays and Saturdays), lunch service until 3pm, then bar. Aperitif from 18 to 20:30. Reservations strongly recommended for lunch, aperitif and dinner.

Located on the tenth floor of Hotel Cavalieri, The Roof gives you a fabulous view of Piazza Missori. While sipping your cocktail, try spotting the domes and bell towers of the nearby Sant'Alessandro church. It is the ideal place to relax and enjoy an aperitif with friends or as a couple.

Reservations can be made for lunch, aperitifs, dinner and after dinner online.

€€€ Organics SkyGarden
Via Giovan Battista Pirelli 20. MM3/MM2 Centrale. Always open 18 - 24, kitchen closes at 22:30.

If you are looking for a green corner in the city, Organics SkyGarden is the place to be. This terrace is located on the 13th floor of the Hyatt Centric Milan

Central hotel. The panoramic view of Milan is simply breathtaking, especially at sunset.

Open daily from 6pm to 10.30pm. DJ Set from 19:30.

€€€€ Sky Terrace
Via dell'Orso 7. MM3 Duomo or MM1 Cordusio or MM2 Lanza. Bar service on the terrace, depending on weather conditions, Tuesday to Saturday, 5pm to 11pm. Online reservation available: check their website.

Sky Terrace, located on the top floor of the Hotel Milano Scala, is an oasis of tranquillity in the heart of the city. With a 360-degree view of Milan, it is the ideal place for a sunset aperitif. The atmosphere is elegant and relaxing, perfect for those seeking a moment of peace away from the chaos of the city.

LUXURY TERRACE RESTAURANTS

€€€€ Torre Restaurant
Via Lorenzini 14. MM3 Lodi. Bar not bookable. Closed Mondays and Tuesdays. Open for dinner only Wednesday, Thursday and Friday, from 7.30pm to midnight. Also open for lunch on Saturdays and Sundays, from 12pm to 3pm. Closed for a few weeks in August and occasionally on other dates, indicated on the website. Online booking available.

If you are looking for a unique experience, **Ristorante Torre** is the place to be. Located on the sixth floor of the Fondazione Prada, it offers a view that embraces the whole of Milan, from CityLife to Gae Aulenti. Here, each dish is a small work of art, perfect for a romantic dinner or a special evening.

€€€€ Giacomo Arengario
Via Guglielmo Marconi 1. MM3 Duomo. Open every day. Aperitif on the terrace only from 4pm to 6pm, not bookable; aperitif at the bar from noon to 11pm. Lunch 12 - 15, dinner 19-24. Online booking available.

The Giacomo Arengario is an institution in Milan. With its terrace overlooking the Duomo, it is the ideal place for a dinner with a breathtaking view. The cuisine is refined and the service impeccable, making every visit an unforgettable experience.

€€€€ Horto
Via San Protaso, 5. MM1 Cordusio. Closed Sundays. From Monday to Saturday, lunch from 12:30 to 14:30, aperitif from 18:30, dinner from 19 to 21:45.

For those who love Mediterranean flavours, **Horto** is an excellent choice, confirmed by 1 Michelin star. Situated in a prime location, it offers fresh and tasty dishes in a relaxed and cosy ambience. Perfect for an evening with friends or a romantic dinner.

Online booking available. In case of problems, the reservation must be cancelled at least 48 hours in advance or 100 euros per person will be charged.

Dinners and aperitifs on the terrace: cheaper options

Milan is famous for its panoramic terraces, but not all of them require a high budget. Here are some options that will allow you to enjoy the city from above without emptying your wallet.

€€ Enosteria Sociale
Via Pietro Calvi 1. Aperitif, dinner or after dinner.

Closed Mondays. Opening at 6 pm and closing at midnight, postponed to 1 am Thursday, Friday, and Saturday.

Enosteria Sociale is the ideal place for wine lovers. This venue offers a selection of natural wines that you can enjoy while listening to live concerts. The atmosphere is cosy and informal, perfect for an evening with friends.

You can book online, choosing between ground floor, first floor or the terrace.

€€ Clotilde Brera
Piazza San Marco 6. MM2 Lanza or MM3 Montenapoleone. Lunch from Monday to Sunday 12:30 - 3 pm. Aperitif or dinner from Monday to Saturday 6 - 10:30 pm. Closed Sunday dinner.

Located in the heart of Brera, Clotilde Brera is an oasis of charm and tranquillity. Here you can enjoy an aperitif or dinner in an elegant and relaxed atmosphere. The view over the rooftops of Milan and the intimate atmosphere make this place perfect for a romantic evening. Reservations can be made online.

WHERE TO BUY A PANETTONE?

Milanese cuisine does not have a long tradition of sweets, but two stand out: the legendary panettone and the Barbajada.

The **Barbajada** is a drink with chocolate, cream, and coffee that originated in the 19th century at the Caffè Cambiasi, which was located next to La Scala Theatre. It was a sweet created to refresh and warm the voice of the artists from the bitter cold of Milan, before the performance. An old-fashioned but nonetheless delicious drink.

Panettone, famous also abroad, is Milan's iconic Christmas cake: a sweet leavened pastry embellished with sultanas and candied fruit, whose name panettone derives from 'pan di Toni', a cake created by Ludovico il Moro's kitchen boy on Christmas Eve to make up for the official dessert that had burnt.

Here are the addresses of some pastry shops where you can buy a well-made panettone. Of course, you usually only find it at Christmas time:

- Pasticceria Martesana, via Cagliero 14;
- Pasticceria Cova, Via Monte Napoleone 8;
- Pasticceria Cucchi, Corso Genova 1;
- Pasticceria Buonarroti, Via Buonarroti 9.

Where to eat a good ice cream

Just as with the best pizza, when it comes to choosing the best ice cream in Milan you'll never find a unanimous judgement.

Italians often have conflicting ideas about ice cream. Some like it creamier, some like it sweeter, some prefer the classic flavours, some look for imaginative and creative flavours.

In any case, 'gelato' is not the same as 'ice cream': in Italy we use milk, not cream.

Here are some of our favourite places and some recommended by internet users. Check opening times on Google: many ice cream parlours have reduced hours in the winter months.

Antica Gelatoria Sartori, Piazza Duca d'Aosta on the corner of Via Pergolesi, MM2/MM3 Centrale

A historic Milanese ice cream parlour, right in the square of the Central Station car park. The granitas are also excellent.

Artico, Via Luigi Porro Lambertenghi 15, MM5 Isola. Several locations in the city!

This ice cream parlour has several shops in the city, check on Google if you have an 'Artico Gelateria' near you. Very popular with both Milanese and tourists, in summer you may find a queue. Dozens of flavours available.

Il Massimo del Gelato, via Lodovico Castelvetro 18, MM5 Gerusalemme

Many flavours of ice cream, with a wide selection of chocolates and creams. They also offer some cold desserts. In the summer months, there's a queue outside.

Gusto 17, via Savona 17, MM2 Porta Genova (Navigli)

One of the best ice cream parlours on the Navigli, according to online reviews. Wide choice of flavours.

Terra, via Vitruvio 38, MM2/MM3 Centrale - MM1 Lima. It also has other locations in the city.

High quality ice cream for a brand that has been gaining popularity for some years now.

WHERE TO GO OUT AT NIGHT IN MILAN

NAVIGLI: THE BEATING HEART OF MILANESE NIGHTLIFE

The Navigli are the true heart of Milan's movida. This area, characterised by its picturesque canals, is the ideal place for those who want to experience an unforgettable evening in Milan.

In the evening, the Navigli turns into a lively meeting place for young people and tourists, offering a wide range of clubs and activities for all tastes.

BRERA: BETWEEN ART AND COCKTAILS

Brera is Milan's artistic quarter, a stone's throw from the centre. With its bohemian and youthful atmosphere, it is the perfect place for those seeking a mix of culture and fun.

Its narrow, cosy streets are ideal for an evening stroll, perhaps after visiting the famous Brera Art Gallery or La Scala Theatre.

CORSO COMO AND GARIBALDI: GLAMOROUS MILAN

If you are looking for a place to start the evening in style, Corso Como is the perfect place. Here you will find trendy cocktail bars offering sophisticated drinks and a chic atmosphere. It is not uncommon to meet VIPs and celebrities while sipping a cocktail outside. The area is pedestrianised, so you can stroll leisurely between bars. Nightlife in Corso Como and Garibaldi is synonymous with unbridled fun.

For a truly unforgettable evening, you cannot miss the rooftop bars with city views. These venues offer a breathtaking view of the Milan skyline, perfect for a sunset aperitif or a drink under the stars. The combination of good music, excellent drinks and a spectacular view makes these bars the ideal place to end your evening on a high note.

In Corso Como, especially at night, remember to take care of your safety: keep your guard up and avoid possible dangers.

Isola: the trendy and alternative district

Isola is an ever-changing neighbourhood that is emerging as one of Milan's new nightlife destinations. Here you will find a selection of trendy bars, craft breweries and clubs with a lively atmosphere. Isola is an up-and-coming area of Milan that is attracting more and more young and creative people.

Porta Romana: the underground soul of Milan

Porta Romana is the perfect place for an alternative night out in Milan. Here you will find clubs with live music ranging from rock to the 80s. Many of these venues have distinctive furnishings and a unique atmosphere. The area is mainly frequented by young people, thanks to the presence of many university students.

Porta Romana is famous for its live music venues. If you prefer a more underground atmosphere, Porta Romana has a lot to offer. The clubs in the area are known for their alternative music and distinctive décor. Here you can find everything from lounge bars to trendy bars, perfect for a night out.

For a quieter evening, you can opt for one of the historic breweries or pubs in the area.

IDROSCALO: THE SEA OF MILAN

Idroscalo is the perfect place for a summer evening out. Known as the 'sea of Milan', this place offers a unique and relaxing atmosphere. Originally a stopover for seaplanes, today it is a large green area with a water basin where you can find outdoor clubs and discos. Although access to the Idroscalo is limited to summer, the surrounding area is full of restaurants and bars open all year round.

What to visit in Milan

The History of Milan at a glance

Milan, a city rich in history and culture, has gone through many transformations over the centuries. Founded by the Insubri Gauls, it became an important Roman city and later a capital of the Western Roman Empire. During the Middle Ages, Milan was the scene of barbarian invasions and foreign domination, until it became a leading economic and cultural centre. Its history continues to influence the present, making it a fascinating and dynamic city.

In a nutshell

- Milan was founded by the Insubri Gauls and became Mediolanum under the Romans.

- During the Roman Empire, Milan became the capital of the Western Roman Empire.

- In the Middle Ages, Milan suffered barbarian invasions and was ruled by the Lombards and the Visconti.

- The modern age saw Milan under foreign domination, including Spanish and Napoleonic rule.

- In the 20th century, Milan was severely damaged during the Second World War but quickly recovered, becoming an economic and cultural centre.

The Origins of Milan

You can find out more about this period of the city at the Archaeological Museum.

Foundation by the Insubri Gauls

Milan was founded by the Insubri Gauls around 590 BC. This Celtic people chose an area near a sanctuary to establish their settlement, which they called Medhelan. Archaeological evidence from the 19th century shows that Milan began as a small village, which gradually grew over time.

Roman conquest and the birth of Mediolanum

In 222 BC, Roman legions conquered Milan, which was renamed Mediolanum. The ancient name of Milan is attested as Mediolanum in ancient Latin written sources. Despite an attempted rebellion by allying with Carthage, the Romans retained control of the city. By the end of the 1st century AD, Milan was an integral part of Roman rule.

Strategic and commercial importance

Thanks to its geographical location, Milan became an important strategic and commercial centre. In fact, the city was in an ideal position for trade and communication, facilitating its economic and urban development.

Milan in the Roman Empire

To learn more about this period, you can read our Tour of Roman Milan.

Capital of the Western Roman Empire

In 286 A.D., Emperor Diocletian decided to move the capital of the Western Roman Empire from Rome to Mediolanum, today's Milan. This choice was dictated by the city's strategic location, which allowed for more effective control of the northern provinces threatened by barbarian invasions. Mediolanum thus became the political and administrative heart of the Empire, with a series of monumental buildings testifying to its importance.

Edict of Milan and religious tolerance

In 313 A.D., Emperor Constantine and his co-emperor Licinius promulgated the Edict of Milan, a document that guaranteed religious freedom to all citizens of the Empire. This edict marked a historical turning point, as it allowed Christians to practise their faith freely without fear of persecution. Mediolanum thus became a centre of great importance for Christianity, attracting numerous believers and religious figures.

Urban and architectural development

During the imperial period, Mediolanum saw considerable urban and architectural development. The city was surrounded by a double circle of walls and within it were prestigious buildings such as the circus, the theatre and the Herculean baths. The main streets, such as today's Via Manzoni, were well-structured and interconnected, facilitating trade and mobility. The city expanded well beyond the Augustan walls, reaching as far as the modern Cerchia dei Navigli road circle.

THE MIDDLE AGES IN MILAN

The Barbarian Invasions

During the Middle Ages, Milan suffered numerous barbarian invasions. In 452, the city was sacked by the Huns, causing severe damage. Later, in 539, the Ostrogoths conquered Milan, bringing further devastation. These events deeply marked the city, which had to face periods of reconstruction and adaptation.

The rule of the Lombards

In 569, the Lombards took control of Milan, marking the beginning of a new chapter in the city's history. During this period, Milan lost part of its importance to Pavia, which became the new capital of Lombardy. However, the city continued to be an important centre, especially because of its strategic and commercial position.

The Visconti-Sforza Seigniory

With the advent of the Visconti Seigniory, Milan experienced a period of great development. The Visconti, a powerful noble family, succeeded in consolidating their power and turning Milan into one of the most influential cities in medieval Italy. During their rule, numerous buildings and fortifications were constructed, including the imposing Castello Sforzesco, which is still one of the main symbols of the city today.

The Modern Age and Foreign Domination

Spanish domination

In 1535, with the death of Francesco II Sforza without an heir, the Duchy of Milan was annexed to the Spanish Empire. This marked the beginning of a long period of Spanish rule that lasted until 1713. During these years, Milan suffered oppressive control both ideologically and fiscally. However, the city also experienced a period of growth thanks to the irrigation of the Po River and the wool and silk trade.

The reforms of Maria Theresa of Austria

In 1713, with the Treaty of Utrecht, the Duchy of Milan came under Austrian control. Maria Theresa of Austria initiated a series of reforms that completely transformed the city. These included the foundation of the Teatro alla Scala and the Braidense National Library. Milan became a leading cultural and artistic centre with a strong urban development.

The Napoleonic occupation

In 1797, Napoleon's troops entered Milan, turning it into the capital of the Cisalpine Republic. Napoleon proclaimed himself King of Italy in 1805 and Milan became the heart of his reign. During this period, the city experienced a cultural and economic renaissance, with important architectural and urban planning works.

The Risorgimento and the Unification of Italy

The Five Days of Milan

During the Risorgimento, Milan was the scene of crucial events. Among these, the Five Days of Milan (18-22 March 1848) represent one of the most significant moments. In those days, the city rose up against Austrian rule and temporarily succeeded in freeing itself. This episode is remembered as a symbol of resistance and desire for freedom for the whole of Italy.

Milan's role in the Risorgimento

Milan played a central role in the Italian Risorgimento. The city was a focal point for the patriotic movements that aimed at the unification of Italy. Revolts and conspiracies against the Austrians, such as the one in 1853, showed how strong the feeling of independence was. Milan became a symbol of the struggle for freedom and national unity.

Annexation to the Kingdom of Italy

After the Second War of Independence and the Peace of Zurich of 1859, Milan and Lombardy were annexed to the Kingdom of Sardinia, which in 1861 became the Kingdom of Italy. This transition marked the end of Austrian rule and the beginning of a new era for the city and the entire nation. Milan, with its history of resistance and patriotism, was fundamental in the process of Italian unification.

Milan in the 20th century

On this period, you will find the Tour of 20th Century Milan on the following pages.

The bombings of the Second World War

During the Second World War, Milan suffered severe bombing damage. Many monuments were damaged and some completely destroyed. The city, however, managed to recover quickly.

The post-war economic miracle

In 1946, Milan began a period of strong economic and commercial development. This led the city to become the hub of Italy's financial and economic activity. Milan led the country's industrial development, forming with Turin and Genoa the 'Industrial Triangle'.

The years of lead and the Milan of drinking

Between the 1970s and 1980s, Milan experienced a period of great turmoil. On the one hand, there were the 'anni di piombo', characterised by political and social tensions. On the other, the 1980s saw the birth of the 'Milano da bere', an era of opulence and fashion that transformed the city into one of the world's leading industry hubs.

The must-sees: what to see in Milan in a day

Are you in Milan for a short time and want to see as much of the city as possible? Here are the places you must see if you are visiting Milan for a day or a weekend.

Depending on the time you have available, you can choose whether to take your time and also visit the inside of some monuments and churches, or to go quickly. As always, we advise you to get help from Google Maps, or a similar app, setting destinations as you go.

Start in **Piazza Duomo** (Duomo metro stop on the 1, Red, and 3, Yellow lines).

The **Duomo of Milan** is the symbol of the city. Entrance is chargeable. If you are in a hurry, you can look at the Lombard Gothic style of the façade, trying to guess the shape of the spires. You can also walk around the church and peer upwards to see the Madonnina, the statue soaring on the highest spire.

Next to the Duomo **Galleria Vittorio Emanuele** is a covered passage with luxury shops and restaurants, literally the heart of Milan. Look around, including upwards, to see the decorations. When you reach the centre of the Galleria, don't forget to look for the representation of the bull on the floor. You might see someone pirouetting on the testicles (represented) of the bull: it is considered a gesture that attracts good luck.

Piazza della Scala, on the other side of the Galleria from the Duomo, is home to the famous La Scala theatre, a temple of opera and classical music, a statue dedicated to Leonardo da Vinci and several period buildings. Not that much to see if you don't have a lot of time.

Piazza Cairoli is one of the points of passage if you are visiting the centre. This square is home to the Starbucks Brewery, a temple of American-style coffee housed in a historic Milanese building. You are in one of the most famous squares of Milanese finance, with the historic headquarters of Assicurazioni Generali, the international bank UniCredit, and the Italian Post Office.

From Piazza Cairoli, take Via Dante and walk to the **Castello Sforzesco**. It can be freely visited in its outdoor areas. It houses some museums (see *Castello Sforzesco Museums* later in this guide) for a fee. Beyond the Castle you will find Parco Sempione, one of the largest and liveliest green areas in the city.

Leonardo da Vinci's Last Supper is probably one of the most famous works of art in the world, also iconic in popular culture. **The Last Supper** is located next to the **Church of Santa Maria alle Grazie**, right next to the Castello Sforzesco. The exact address is Piazza di Santa Maria alle Grazie 2.

Remember: **admission to the Cenacolo is subject to payment and reservation. You should book as early as possible.** In high season, even weeks or months in advance.

If you haven't booked, though, try anyway. Go to the ticket office at the opening or around closing time, when it is more likely that there is some admission available. Or that someone booked and... didn't show up. The visit lasts about 15 minutes, admissions are based on shifts. Try to get to the ticket office early so you don't miss your turn.

Now you can move by underground (or taxi, or just walk there) to **Piazza Gae Aulenti** in the **Porta Nuova** district is the heart of the 'new' Milan. Modern buildings and architecture house the offices of large companies and shops. It is impossible not to notice the UniCredit Tower towering above you. There are several places in the Piazza where you can have a coffee, an ice cream or a quick snack.

If you are short of time, you can walk from Piazza Gae Aulenti to the Passerella Gioia, taking advantage of a pedestrian area where you can see numerous interesting buildings. The IBM Studios, for example, is a building resembling a wooden basket, where private events are held: it cannot be visited.

Above all, on your left you should see the two residential buildings of the **Bosco Verticale** (Vertical Garden). These are private residences that are distinguished by the presence of trees throughout their height. An architectural masterpiece. Not surprisingly, they are one of the most photographed places in Milan.

Do you still have time? Then keep walking. You can walk towards the two buildings of the Giardino Verticale, to see them up close and enjoy the surrounding park, called the **Libreria degli Alberi** (Library of Trees). In front of you lies the Isola district, a resounding case of real estate revaluation in recent years.

If you are staying for the evening or the night, you can have an aperitivo or dinner in the **Navigli** area (from Piazza XXIV Maggi), or in **Brera**.

THE UNMISSABLE WORKS OF ART IN MILAN

THE LAST SUPPER BY LEONARDO DA VINCI

- Church of Santa Maria delle Grazie

Leonardo da Vinci's Last Supper, also known as The Last Supper, is one of the world's most famous masterpieces. Created between 1495 and 1498, this wall painting is located in the refectory of the convent of Santa Maria delle Grazie in Milan. Commissioned by Ludovico il Moro, it depicts the moment when Jesus announces the betrayal of one of his disciples. The work is famous for its ability to capture the emotions and reactions of the apostles, making it an icon of Renaissance art.

Techniques used by Leonardo

Leonardo did not use the traditional fresco technique for the Last Supper, but experimented with a dry technique using pigments spread on a white preparatory layer. This method, although innovative, made the work vulnerable to time and humidity in the refectory. A few years after its completion, the painting began to deteriorate, requiring numerous restorations. Today, thanks to a significant restoration in 1977, we can still admire this masterpiece, albeit in a less brilliant form than the original.

How to book a visit

Visiting the Cenacolo Vinciano is an unmissable experience for anyone in Milan. However, due to its popularity, tickets must be booked well in advance. Visits are organised in small groups to preserve the work and ensure a more intimate experience. You can book tickets online at the Cenacolo Vinciano's official website or through authorised agencies. Don't miss the opportunity to see one of the greatest masterpieces of art history up close!

THE KISS BY FRANCESCO HAYEZ

- Brera Art Gallery

"Hayez's 'The Kiss' is more than just a portrait of two lovers. Painted in 1859, this painting has become a symbol of the Italian Risorgimento. Set in a medieval era, the painting conceals a message of rebellion against the foreign occupation in Italy. The kiss between the two young people represents love for the homeland and the fight for the unification of Italy.

Symbolism and interpretations

Behind the apparent simplicity of the kiss, numerous symbols are concealed. The dagger hidden under the cloak and the suspicious shadow in the background are details that suggest a context of conspiracy and resistance. This painting is not only a romantic icon, but also a powerful political message.

Where to admire it

If you want to see 'The Kiss' in person, you have to go to the Pinacoteca di Brera. This museum houses the original of the painting, donated by Count Alfonso Maria Visconti in 1886. The Pinacoteca di Brera is one of the most fascinating places in Milan, and a visit here is a must for any art lover.

DEAD CHRIST BY ANDREA MANTEGNA

- Brera Art Gallery

Andrea Mantegna's Dead Christ is one of the most impressive and revolutionary works of the Renaissance. Conserved in the Pinacoteca di Brera, this painting, created between 1475 and 1478, depicts the body of Christ lying on a stone slab, covered by a sheet. The particularity of the work lies in the point of view chosen by Mantegna: Christ is seen in foreshortening, creating a perspective effect that immediately captures the viewer's attention.

The use of perspective

Mantegna used a bold and innovative perspective for his time. The body of Christ is represented in such a way that it appears to extend towards the observer, an effect that accentuates the drama and solemnity of the scene. This use of perspective is one of the elements that make the Dead Christ a masterpiece of great technical and artistic achievement.

The Impact on Renaissance Art

Mantegna's work had a significant impact on Renaissance art. His ability to combine realism and perspective influenced many later artists. The Dead Christ is not only a work of art, but also a profound reflection on death and suffering, expressed with an emotional force that continues to touch anyone who observes it.

MICHELANGELO'S PIETÀ RONDANINI

- Castello Sforzesco Museums

The Pietà Rondanini is the last sculpture created by Michelangelo Buonarroti. Begun in 1552 and reworked until 1564, shortly before his death, this sculpture represents a tormented and unfinished work. Michelangelo wanted to create a Pietà for his burial, but the project underwent numerous changes over the years. The statue shows Jesus in the arms of Mary, but with an innovative fusion of the two bodies that expresses a profound union between mother and son.

The significance of the Pieta

This work is a testament to Michelangelo's final meditation on death and the salvation of the soul. Unlike his previous works, here the artist renounces the perfection of the human body to represent suffering and fragility. The dead Christ becomes a symbol of pain, striking for its modernity and emotional intensity. The Pietà Rondanini is a masterpiece that reflects Michelangelo's inner conflict and his struggle with matter.

Its location in the Castello Sforzesco

Today, the Pietà Rondanini is kept in the Museum of the Castello Sforzesco in Milan. Originally, the work was located in the Palazzo Rondanini in Rome, from which it takes its name. In 1952, the sculpture was moved to Milan, where it has become one of the museum's main attractions. If you visit Milan, you cannot miss the opportunity to admire this extreme masterpiece by Michelangelo, which continues to inspire and move visitors from all over the world.

UNIQUE FORMS OF CONTINUITY IN SPACE BY UMBERTO BOCCIONI

- Museo del Novecento, Piazza del Duomo

Futurism was a revolutionary artistic movement, and Umberto Boccioni was one of its main exponents. Born in 1882, Boccioni sought to capture the dynamism and energy of modern life. His most famous work, 'Unique Forms of Continuity in Space', perfectly represents these ideals. Created in 1913, this sculpture is an icon of Futurism and can be found at the Museo del Novecento in Milan.

Analysis of the work

'Unique Forms of Continuity in Space' is a sculpture that seems almost to be in motion. Its fluid and dynamic lines give the impression of a body moving forward in space, breaking with the static tradition of classical sculpture. The work is so representative of the movement, that it was chosen for the reverse side of the 20 cent euro coins minted in Italy. Observing it closely, one can see the expressive details that make this sculpture unique.

Where to find it

If you want to see this extraordinary work live, you must visit the Museo del Novecento in Milan. Located in Piazza del Duomo, the museum houses a vast collection of 20th century art, with a section dedicated to Futurism. Here, you can see 'Unique Forms of Continuity in Space' and other works by Boccioni up close, fully immersing yourself in the energy and vitality of the Futurist movement.

THE SEVEN HEAVENLY PALACES BY ANSELM KIEFER

- Hangar Bicocca
- free visit

Since 2004, Anselm Kiefer's Seven Heavenly Palaces have been a permanent presence at the Hangar Bicocca in Milan. This monumental installation consists of seven reinforced concrete towers, between 14 and 18 metres high. The work is a mix of heaviness and lightness, recalling symbols of the Jewish mystical tradition and ancient civilisations.

Symbolism and meaning

The installation takes its name from the Sefer Hechalot, an ancient Jewish text describing a spiritual journey towards the divine. The towers represent this journey, with each element symbolising a step towards knowledge and spirituality. Kiefer used materials such as concrete and lead to create a work that is both solid and fragile.

Guided tours and timetables

You can visit the installation for free at Hangar Bicocca. Guided tours are available and offer a unique opportunity to better understand the deeper meaning of the work. Opening hours vary, so it is always best to check the official website before planning your visit.

Caravaggio's Basket of Fruit

- Pinacoteca Ambrosiana

Caravaggio's Basket of Fruit is an iconic painting, preserved at the Pinacoteca Ambrosiana in Milan. Painted between 1594 and 1598, this masterpiece is a perfect example of Caravaggio's realism. Caravaggio, with his extraordinary skill, manages to render every detail of the fruit and the wicker basket with incredible precision. The leaves pierced by insects and the dried twigs almost seem to come out of the painting, creating a breathtaking three-dimensional effect.

Detailed analysis of the painting

In this painting, Caravaggio celebrates the imperfect beauty of nature. The fruit, with its imperfections and signs of decay, represents the fragility and transience of human life. This concept is further emphasised by the wicker basket, which seems almost about to give way under the weight of the fruit. The Basket of Fruit is considered one of the most emblematic still lifes in art history, a work that revolutionised the genre and influenced countless subsequent artists.

The Pinacoteca Ambrosiana and its works

The Pinacoteca Ambrosiana is one of Milan's most important museums and houses a vast collection of artworks, including Caravaggio's famous Canestra di Frutta (Basket of Fruit). Founded in 1618 by Cardinal Federico Borromeo, the picture gallery is a must-see for art lovers. In addition to the Basket of Fruit, here you can admire masterpieces by artists such as

Leonardo da Vinci, Raphael, and Botticelli. A visit to the Pinacoteca Ambrosiana is a journey through centuries of art history, an enriching and inspiring experience.

Milan area by area: what to see

The centre and the cathedral area

The Duomo

The Duomo of Milan is the city's iconic monument. Until a few years ago, the visit was free of charge, but nowadays, there is a charge, except for the faithful who want to attend mass.

There are many versions of the tickets. Here are the main ones:

- 30 euro Fast Track Pass all-inclusive, including lift to terraces
- 25 euros for Cathedral, Terraces with lift, Cathedral Museum and St Gotthard Church
- 20 euros for Cathedral, Terraces Walk, Cathedral Museum and St Gotthard Church
- 10 euros Cathedral and museum
- 34 euro combo Pinacoteca Ambrosiana + Duomo, Terrazze a Piedi, Museo del Duomo, Chiesa San Gottardo, Archaeological Area

On Wednesdays, only the Duomo ticket can be purchased. The 20, 25 and 30 euro tickets are valid for three days.

Opening hours:

Cathedral, daily from 10 a.m. to 4.10 p.m.

The Cathedral Museum Thursday to Tuesday from 10 a.m. to 7 p.m., closed on Wednesdays

At a glance: what to see

- The Gothic-style façade with spires, statues, and decorations: if you buy a ticket for the Terraces, you can see some of them up close
- The interior stained-glass windows, created in different periods by Lombard, Italian, and international artists
- The many statues and works of art inside
- In the last bay before the altar, the work Saint Ambrose Imposing Penance and Theodosius by Federico Barocci of 1603
- Above the high altar, suspended and attached to the keystone, is the Holy Nail, which tradition says is one of the four nails used for the crucifixion of Jesus Christ
- The crypt

More detailed description

The Cathedral has a surface area of 11,700 square metres, while its largest spire reaches 108.5 metres. It was on this spire that the Madonnina, a statue representing the Madonna by sculptor Giuseppe Perego, was placed in 1774.

It is built in the Lombard Gothic style, which combines the characteristics of international Gothic with some peculiarities of Lombardy, in a riot of spires, pinnacles, statues, cornices, sculptures and meticulous decoration.

The plan of the church is in the shape of a Latin cross. The terraces of the cathedral can be visited for a fee: access is by stairs or a lift and from the top there is a beautiful view of the city.

The construction of Milan Cathedral began in 1386, on sacred ground where the basilicas of Santa Tecla and Santa Maria Maggiore once stood. Strongly desired by Gian Galeazzo Visconti, the Duomo was built to celebrate the lordship of the Visconti family, to provide a place of worship in the centre of the city and to pay homage to Maria Nascente.

The construction of the cathedral took centuries and, as a Milanese expression goes, is never actually finished, as maintenance and renovation of individual parts is constantly being carried out. The building is made entirely of an exclusive white-golden marble from the Candoglia quarries in the Ossola Valley.

In November, the Quadroni di San Carlo, large paintings illustrating the life of Saint Ambrose, are exhibited inside.

Piazza del Duomo

In Piazza del Duomo, the beating heart of Milan, there are many interesting buildings. On the square is the monument to Victor Emmanuel II, a bronze statue representing the first King of Italy on horseback during the Battle of San Martino. The statue was placed in the square in 1896.

Around the square we find:

- Palazzo Carminati, a pink building opposite the cathedral;
- the southern arcades, on the left, with the Torre dell'Arengario. On this side are also the Museo del Novecento and the Palazzo Reale, home to important art exhibitions;

- the northern arcades, to the right, lead to the entrance of the Galleria Vittorio Emanuele and, a little further on, provide access to the Rinascente, the city's iconic shopping centre.

GALLERIA VITTORIO EMANUELE

The Galleria Vittorio Emanuele II is a covered and prestigious passage connecting Piazza Duomo with Piazza della Scala. Inside are clubs, bars, restaurants and luxury boutiques of the most important fashion labels.

The Galleria dates back to the 19th century and was created to connect Piazza Duomo to Piazza della Scala, initially only a wide and convenient road was planned, which later evolved into a tunnel.

A 'fashionable passage', with a glass and iron roof, inspired by the famous Galerie Vivienne in Paris and Burlington Arcade in London.

The Galleria Vittorio Emanuele consists of a main arm (196.6 metres) connecting the two prestigious squares, and a short arm (105.1 metres). At their intersection is the dome, made of iron and glass, which creates a very evocative atmosphere.

In the central part, from where the four arms start, we can look up to see four coats of arms or lunettes in the corners, in which the four continents are depicted: Europe, America, Asia, and Africa. The paintings were created by four different painters: Casnedi, Pagliano, Giuliano and Pietrasanta.

If we look down again, we see that the floor of the Gallery is made of marble, in the part at the dome we find mosaics depicting the coat of arms of the Savoy family and on the sides, there are the coats of arms of the cities that at different times were the capitals of the Kingdom of Italy: Milan, Turin, Florence, and Rome.

One curiosity concerns Turin's coat of arms. Legend has it that it brings good luck to rest the heel of the right foot on the bull's genitals and turn around three times. It is not at all uncommon to find tourists repeating this gesture. In fact, as you will see, the pavement at the bull's genitals is completely worn.

THE MUSEO DEL NOVECENTO (XXTH CENTURY ARTS)

The Museo del Novecento is located inside the Palazzo dell'Arengario (Via Marconi 1), overlooking the Piazza del Duomo.

Tickets

Full price 5 euro, reduced 3 euro, free for some categories and conventions

Admission is included in the Museo Abbonamenti Lombardia, both versions of the YesMilano City Pass, the Milano Museo Card and the Tourist Museum Card.

Timetable

Closed Mondays. Open Tuesday to Sunday 10 am - 7.30 pm. Thursday closing at 22:30. Last admission one hour before closing.

The Museo del Novecento was opened in 2010 to present 20th century art, especially Italian art. It houses around 400 works inside the historic Palazzo dell'Arengario.

What not to miss:

- Futurism, an Italian art movement of the 20th century, with works by Umberto Boccioni, Giacomo Balla, Carlo Carrà, Ardengo Soffici, Mario Sironi, Gino Severini and Achille Funi;
- Giorgio de Chirico's Metaphysics, Lucio Fontana's cuts, Giorgio Morandi's works;
- the work The Fourth Estate by Giuseppe Pellizza da Volpedo, a symbol of the struggles of the working class;
- the works of Pablo Picasso, Georges Braque, Kandinsky and Amedeo Modigliani.

Piazza della Scala

If we continue along the long arm of the Galleria, we come to Piazza della Scala. It was built in 1858 to create space in front of the famous La Scala theatre, literally one of the temples of opera, music, and ballet.

In addition to the theatre, the square also contains Palazzo Marino, which is opposite, and the two buildings of the Banca Commerciale Italiana, one of which houses the Gallerie d'Italia museum in Milan.

In the centre of the Piazza is the Monument to Leonardo da Vinci, created by sculptor Pietro Magni and inaugurated in 1872. The figure of Leonardo stands out, but below him are his four Milanese pupils: Marco d'Oggiono, Gian Giacomo Caprotti, Cesare da Sesto and Giovanni Antonio Boltraffio.

The arrangement of the five statues is reminiscent of a bottle of wine with four glasses around it, and has been jokingly dubbed 'on litre in quater' by the Milanese, meaning one litre in four.

Also worth mentioning is the Monument to Giulio Ricordi, a very recent work by Luigi Secchi that was inaugurated in 2016.

Also in the square, for fans of Leonardo Da Vinci, the Museo Leonardo 3 displays reconstructions of some machines of the great Italian Renaissance genius.

GALLERIE D'ITALIA (ART MUSEM)

Piazza della Scala, 6. Open Tuesday to Sunday 9:30 am - 7:30 pm, Thursday closing at 10:30 pm. The ticket office closes one hour before. Full price ticket 10 euro, reduced price ticket over65 8 euro, reduced price ticket under 26 and Intesa Sanpaolo Group customers 5 euro. Free for under18. Free entrance on the first Sunday of the month. Museum included in the Musei Lombardia season ticket.

The Gallerie d'Italia is an exhibition complex belonging to the Intesa Sanpaolo bank, with branches in other Italian cities as well. In Milan there are both permanent collections and temporary exhibitions.

The works on display range from the 19th to the 20th century. They include:

- plaster bas-reliefs by Canova;
- the many works on Italian Romanticism, with Francesco Hayez, Giovanni Migliara and other authors;

- patriotic works from the period of the Italian Risorgimento, including those by Gerolamo Induno and Sebastiano De Albertis;
- the opportunity to gain an insight into the tastes of the period, including Lombard landscapes, revival of the 18th century style, Flemish-inspired genre painting, and Alpine painting;
- the works of Symbolism and Futurism, in which Boccioni stands out.

For those who have time on their hands, the explanatory panels in the various rooms give a very clear idea of the art and tastes of the 19th and 20th centuries.

LEONARDO MUSEUM 3

Piazza della Scala, entrance from Galleria Vittorio Emanuele II. Open daily, 9.30am-9pm. Full price 15 euro, reduced price over65 and students 11 euro, children between 6 and 18 years 9 euro. There is a family ticket for 2 adults and 2 children between 6 and 15 years, 38 euros. Museum included in the Abbonamento Musei Lombardia.

This museum started as a temporary exhibition, which later became permanent. It does not contain Leonardo's paintings, but reconstructions of some of the machines he designed, such as the Mechanical Eagle, the Great Kite, the Fast Crossbow, the Time Machine, the Clavi-Viola, the Musical Cannon, the Spring-engined Screw, the Submarine and the Giant Trumpet.

One can browse digital versions of his manuscripts and view digital restorations of his most important works, including the Last Supper.

LA RINASCENTE SHOPPING MALL

From Piazza Duomo, it may be worth making a trip to the Rinascente, a place of worship for all fashion enthusiasts, inside which the collections of the biggest Italian and international luxury brands are housed.

The history of La Rinascente began in Milan in 1865 when brothers Luigi and Ferdinando Bocconi opened the first Italian shop dedicated to ready-made clothes.

In 1917 Senator Borletti took over the shop and entrusted the poet Gabriele D'Annunzio with the search for a name. D'Annunzio chose 'Rinascente' as the shop's symbol of rebirth. On Christmas night in 1918, the shop was destroyed by fire and only reopened in March 1921.

In this shop, it is possible to buy clothing for men, women and children, there are accessories, shoes, bags, beauty products, cosmetics, perfumes, and even household products. Inside the Rinascente you can find various bars and restaurants ready to satisfy every need, from coffee to sushi, from meat to focaccia, for an exclusive aperitif we recommend Il Bar on the terrace overlooking the Duomo.

PIAZZA DEI MERCANTI AND SURROUNDINGS

A stone's throw from the cathedral, it is a historical medieval square where trade used to take place. It is surrounded by some interesting buildings, such as the

Palazzo della Ragione and the Loggia degli Osii. Not historical, but still indicative of the city's evolution over time, is the secondary entrance to a McDonald's.

Via Dante is a historic connecting street, full of shops and interesting buildings.

Piazza Cordusio, near the Duomo, is surrounded by imposing historical buildings, headquarters of large financial companies. A Starbucks Brewery has opened in a former Italian Post Office building, where the American coffee giant pays homage to the Italian espresso tradition with a shop that is also an experiential journey into the world of coffee. Very touristy, but well worth a visit, especially if you fancy a frappuccino.

Piazza degli Affari

Also nearby is the headquarters of the Italian Stock Exchange, Palazzo Mezzanotte, with the famous L.O.V.E. sculpture by Italian artist Maurizio Cattelan. The address to set in your navigator is Piazza degli Affari.

Velasca Tower

A few steps from the Duomo, the Torre Velasca (Piazza Velasca 3/5) is a 26-storey skyscraper built in the 1950s, whose architecture has been the subject of debate for decades: symbol of the city or element of ugliness?

Designed between 1950 and 1955 and built between 1956 and 1958 (in 292 days, 8 less than the planned time), it has a 'mushroom' shape with the upper part larger than the lower part, which we can consider the base.

It was built in a style defined as 'neo-liberty', which on the one hand looked back to the past and the palaces of the 19th century, and on the other aimed at economic momentum, the future, and innovations. The much derided structure was a true masterpiece for its time, a complex project that was not easy to realise.

The Torre Velasca is featured in the film 'Il Vedovo' by Dino Risi with Alberto Sordi and Franca Valeri, and has been dubbed by the Milanese 'the skyscraper with braces' or 'the skyscraper of braces'. In 2012, 'The Daily Telegraph' listed the Torre Velasca as one of the ugliest buildings in the world. The Torre Velasca is currently used for commercial and residential purposes: the first eighteen floors house shops and offices, from the 19th to the 26th there are flats (there are 800 in total). Unless you know someone who lives there, the tower cannot be visited.

THE PINACOTECA AMBROSIANA

Piazza Pio XI, 2. Open Tuesday to Sunday, 10am to 6pm. Closed Mondays, 25 December, 1 January and Easter. Admission 15 euro, reduced ticket 10 euro for under18, over65 and conventioned. Included in the Abbonamento Musei Lombardia

The Pinacoteca Ambrosiana holds 1,500 works on wood, canvas and copper and about 248 drawings by masters of the calibre of Raphael, Leonardo da Vinci, Caravaggio and Titian.

Founded in 1607 by Cardinal Federico Borromeo as the Biblioteca Ambrosiana, the same Cardinal in 1618 donated his personal collection of paintings, statues, prints, drawings and engravings and established the Pinacoteca Ambrosiana.

It contains over 1,500 works in 24 rooms. These are the ones we think are unmissable:

- the Musician of Leonardo da Vinci
- Caravaggio's Basket of Fruit
- the preparatory cartoon for Raphael's School of Athens
- Titian's Adoration of the Magi
- Botticelli's Madonna of the Pavilion
- the Flower Vases of Jan Brueghel
- Leonardo da Vinci's Codex Atlanticus.

There are also some curiosities, including the gloves that Napoleon wore at Waterloo and a display case containing a lock of Lucrezia Borgia's hair, a source of inspiration for great poets such as Gabriele D'Annunzio and Lord Byron.

WALK FROM THE DUOMO TO SAN BABILA

From Piazza del Duomo, it is possible to continue on foot, behind the cathedral, along Corso Vittorio Emanuele II (always him) to Piazza San Babila, the historic meeting place of paninari in the 1980s.

Here in the square is the Basilica di San Babila, a historic Milanese church that may be worth a visit: see the detailed tour sheet.

Turning left into Piazza San Babila, you can walk along Corso Venezia to the Corso Buenos Aires area, enjoying the parade of historic buildings. See the section North East Milan: what to see.

BRERA DISTRICT

The Brera District lies just west of the Duomo and is roughly bounded by Via Pontaccio, Via Fatebenefratelli, Via dei Giardini, Via Monte di Pietà, Via Ponte Vetero and Via Mercato.

It is one of the city's most charming and romantic neighbourhoods, with museums, markets, the Academy of Fine Arts, bars, restaurants, cafés and a botanical garden.

Every third Sunday of the month, with the exception of August (sorry, summer tourists!) the Brera Market takes place: in Via Brera and Via Fiori Chiari come antique stalls with jewellery, modern antiques and unique, unobtainable objects.

THE BRERA ART GALLERY

Via Brera 28. Tuesday, Wednesday, Thursday, Friday, Saturday and Sunday from 8.30 am to 7.15 pm (ticket office closes at 6.40 pm). Full price ticket 15 euro, reduced price ticket 10 euro. Admission 2 euro for EU citizens, Switzerland, Iceland, Norway and Liechtenstein between 18 and 25 years of age. Free for Italian journalists, foreign journalists must be accredited by email in the days before. Audioguide 2 euros. Free entrance on the first Sunday of the month but online booking remains compulsory. The Pinacoteca di Brera is part of the Abbonamento Musei Lombardia.

Bookings:
https://pinacotecadibrera.eventim-inhouse.de/websho p/webticket/timeslot

On Via Brera is Palazzo di Brera, which is the seat of the Brera Art Gallery, the Academy of Fine Arts, the Braidense National Library, the offices of the Astronomical and Meteorological Observatory and the Botanical Garden, and in which there is a bronze statue by Antonio Canova dedicated to Napoleon I in 1809.

The Pinacoteca di Brera consists of 38 rooms displaying masterpieces by Italian artists from the 14th to the 19th century and some foreign artists, including Piero della Francesca, Mantegna, Raphael, Bramante, Caravaggio, Tintoretto, Bellini, and Bronzino. In the courtyard at the entrance is a work by Canova depicting the effigy of Napoleon.

The unmissable works:

- the flagellation of Christ by Luca Signorelli,
- the Dead Christ by Andrea Mantegna,
- the sacred conversation by Piero della Francesca,
- the Marriage of the Virgin by Raphael,
- the Pietà by Giovanni Bellini,
- The Kiss by Francesco Hayez.

The Castello Sforzesco (Sforza Castle)

The Castello Sforzesco is one of the most important sights in Milan. It was built by Francesco Sforza in the 15th century and is a work of art by Antonio Averlino (known as Il Filarete) brought in especially from Florence.

It is just a few minutes' walk from the Duomo and is immersed in the 47-hectare Sempione Park.

Visits to the courtyards of the Castello Sforzesco are free of charge. An entrance ticket for the Castle Museums must be purchased instead.

After its construction, Ludovico il Moro was responsible for making the Castello Sforzesco even more beautiful thanks to the frescoes by Bramante and Leonardo da Vinci, which can still be admired today in the Sala delle Asse (included in the admission ticket).

In the 16th century, when Milan was under Spanish rule, the Castello Sforzesco became a military citadel and remained so during the Habsburg and Napoleonic periods.

In fact, Napoleon Bonaparte ordered the destruction of the castle but that order, fortunately, was never completed.

In the following decades, the Castle suffered some damage, until it was completely restored in the early 20th century by architect Luca Beltrami, who handed the city of Milan a building very faithful to the original, thanks to careful studies of its structure.

The Castello Sforzesco belongs to the City of Milan and is also home to several important museums: an Art Gallery (not the Brera Art Gallery, but the Pinacoteca del Castello), an Egyptian Museum, a Museum of Ancient Art, a Museum of Musical Instruments, an Art Library, a Historical Archive and a Trivulziana Library.

Occasionally, exhibitions and shows are hosted at the Castello Sforzesco.

THE SFORZA CASTLE MUSEUMS

Inside the Castle. 9 a.m. to 5.30 p.m. Tuesday to Sunday. Last admission at 5 p.m. Closed on Mondays, 25 December, 1 January and 1 May. Full price ticket 5 euro, reduced 3 euro. The Castle museums are included in the Tourist Museum Card and in the Musei Lombardia Milano card.

The Castello Sforzesco houses a number of museums with important works, such as Michelangelo Buonarroti's Pietà Rondanini. They range from art to more specialised subjects, such as decorative arts or musical instruments.

Pinacoteca del Castello: includes 1,500 paintings by the most important painters ranging from the splendours of the Visconti and Sforza courts to works by Foppa, Bergognone, Bramantino, Andrea Mantegna, Antonello da Messina, Daniele Crespi, Carlo Francesco Nuvolone, Sebastiano Ricci, Canaletto, Gianbattista Tiepolo, Francesco Guardi and Bernardo Bellotto.

Pietà Rondanini Museum: housed in the former Castle Hospital, we find here Michelangelo's last masterpiece, the Pietà Rondanini. This unfinished work, made when the artist was an old man, encapsulates the essence of human love from a single block of marble. Michelangelo sculpted the figures of Christ and the Virgin fused in a single embrace.

Museum of Decorative Arts: an exhibition of 1,300 objets d'art in ivory, metal, glass, ceramics, textiles, ranging from the early Middle Ages to the Contemporary Age.

Museum of Musical Instruments: a collection of objects donated by the Monzino family, a historic Milanese factory specialising in musical instruments. In addition to these prestigious gifts, there is a collection of string, plucked and wind instruments dating from the Renaissance to the 20th century. The museum is completed by a collection of musical instruments from various parts of the world.

Museum of Prehistory and Protohistory: an exhibition of objects and materials that reconstruct and tell the story of human life in northern Italy from the Neolithic to the 2nd and 1st centuries BC. C.

Egyptian Museum: a collection of objects that tell the story of Egyptian culture, relics, papyri and decorated wood, divinities, vases, funerary statuettes, amulets, painted sarcophagi and even a mummy from the 7th century B.C. Museum of Ancient Art: a collection of 400 sculptural works that tell the story of Lombardy, from the Middle Ages to the Renaissance.

The Park Sempione

Walking through the inner courtyards of the Castle, one arrives in Parco Sempione, Milan's green lung. A large park in which to stroll and relax, open from early morning to evening.

The park was created at the end of the 19th century, in the area previously occupied by the Piazza d'Armi of the Castello Sforzesco, to which it therefore remains ideally linked. The project was entrusted to the architect Emilio Alemagna, who created an English-style park covering an area of 386,000 square metres.

Since its construction, Sempione Park has been the site of important events such as the International Exhibition of 1906: an Art Nouveau pavilion, restored in 2006, remains. It is located in the northern part of the Park and houses the Civic Aquarium: architecture enthusiasts can appreciate it from the outside. A visit inside, however, is recommended if you are interested in freshwater fish.

Since 1973, Sempione Park has been embellished with a number of works of art that can be encountered while strolling through it: 'History of the Earth' by A. Paradiso, 'Musical Accumulation' by Arman and the 'Mysterious Baths' by Giorgio De Chirico.

Inside Sempione Park you can also see:

- the Palazzo dell'Arte, home of the Triennale, which we will explore shortly;
- the Torre del Parco or Torre Littoria, designed by Giò Ponti in 1932;
- the Park Library, originally a Pavilion for the 10th Triennial Exhibition in 1954;
- sculptures such as the equestrian monument of Napoleon III;
- the Sirenette Bridge by Francesco Tettamanzi, also indicated on Google Maps.

THE TRIENNALE (DESIGN AND CONTEMPORARY ART MUSEUM)

Viale Emilio Alemagna, 6. Every day from Tuesday to Sunday from 10:30 a.m. to 8 p.m. Closed on Mondays. The ticket office closes one hour before. The €25 single ticket allows you to visit all the scheduled exhibitions. Otherwise, you can buy the ticket for each exhibition on the website, the price is variable. Online you can find many reductions and discounts.

The programme of current exhibitions can be found at https://triennale.org/

This exhibition space is dedicated to contemporary art and design. The building was constructed in 1933 to a design by Giovanni Muzio.

In 2007, the Triennale Design Museum was inaugurated, a constantly evolving museum that tells the story of design in all its aspects. In 2011, the Teatro dell'Arte was also created, a place dedicated to important cultural projects, especially those dedicated to the performing arts.

THE ARCO DELLA PACE

Walking through the Sempione park you will arrive at the Arco della Pace, another landmark of Milan, especially its western area. It is located in Piazza Sempione and is surrounded by venues for lunch, aperitifs and evening entertainment.

His story deserves to be told briefly.

The Peace Arch, officially, is a monument dedicated to the peace between European nations that was achieved in 1815 at the Congress of Vienna. It was inaugurated on 10 September 1838 in a ceremony presided over by Emperor Ferdinand I of Austria.

It stands where an initial, temporary, wooden arch was erected by Marquis Cagnola to celebrate the arrival in

Milan of the newlyweds Eugene de Beauharnais, viceroy of Italy, and Augusta of Bavaria.

However, the citizens liked the wooden arch very much and it was therefore decided to build one in Baveno granite and marble from Crevola d'Ossola, to celebrate the French victory at the Battle of Jena. As history lovers will have noticed, we are in the middle of the Napoleonic period, while the Austrians inaugurated the Arch.

Let's see what happened in between. In 1807 work began to build the Arch. The project was overseen by Cagnola and promoted by the City of Milan and Napoleon himself: when the Italic Kingdom and the French fell, however, the work was abandoned and the building site left half-finished. An ugly symbol of decline.

In 1826, Francis I of Austria intervened and the project of the Arch, dedicated to peace, was set in motion again. At its top is the Sestiga della Pace, a six-horse bronze chariot by Abbondio Sangiorgio; in the corners are the four Victories on horseback by Giovanni Putti.

On the front are depictions of the four Lombardy-Veneto rivers: the Po, Ticino, Adda and Tagliamento; above the arch are engraved the names of the fallen of the Second World War, on the side the fallen of the First World War. In the centre is a slab engraved with a dedication to Victor Emmanuel II and next to it are bas-reliefs depicting two soldiers.

The change from French to Austrian control also concerns another curiosity about the Arch of Peace, namely the position of the horses. In the original design they were supposed to look outwards, i.e. towards

Paris. The Austrians rotated them 180° to turn their backs to France!

An anecdote relates to Ernest Hemingway's novel 'Festa Mobile', in which we read that the Arch of Peace in Milan is aligned with the Arc de Triomphe du Carrousel and the Arc de Triomphe de l'Etoile in Paris. This is not actually the case, but many like to think that there is this suggestive connection.

PIAZZALE CADORNA

Close to the Castello Sforzesco is Piazzale Cadorna. This modern, busy square is home to the railway station of the same name (the Malpensa Express, a train connecting Milan and Milan Malpensa Airport, departs from here) and a stop of the Line 2 metro.

At the end of the 20th century, the square was completely redesigned by Gae Aulenti: coloured canopies, pink granite pavements, red columns, green panels, glass roofs and fountains were added.

In the centre of the square is an imposing installation, the sculpture 'Ago e Filo' (Needle and Thread) depicting a giant needle with a thread and a knot: it symbolises Milanese industriousness and was conceived and designed by architects Coosje van Bruggen and Claes Oldenburg.

LEONARDO'S LAST SUPPER (SANTA MARIA DELLE GRAZIE)

Timetable

The Basilica can be freely visited during opening hours.

The Upper Room can be visited daily, Tuesday to Sunday, from 8:15 a.m. to 7 p.m. (last entrance is at 6:45 p.m.).

Be at the ticket office 30 minutes before the booked time. The visit takes place in groups and after 30 minutes you will have to leave.

Tickets

Caution. We will repeat it many times in this guide: the visit to the Last Supper must be booked online, if possible well in advance, and tickets must be collected at the ticket office 30 minutes before the scheduled entrance time.

- 15 euro full ticket
- 2 euros for 18-25 year olds
- Free for visitors under 18 years of age: children under 12 must always be accompanied

On the official website you can book your visit, check prices and updated conventions.

The visit to the Church is free, while there is a separate entrance fee for the Last Supper.

One of the stars of Milan is the Basilica di Santa Maria delle Grazie (address: Piazza di Santa Maria delle Grazie) which houses the Last Supper by Leonardo Da Vinci.

Santa Maria delle Grazie is one of the most important churches in Milan where the Last Supper or The Last Supper, one of Leonardo da Vinci's most important works, is kept.

In 1980, the Church and the Last Supper were declared a UNESCO World Heritage Site.

In 1463, the Duke of Milan, Francesco I Sforza, decided to have a Dominican convent and church built on the site of a chapel dedicated to Santa Maria delle Grazie. The convent was completed in 1469 and the church a few years later, in 1482. The church was later modified at the behest of the Duke of Milan, Ludovico il Moro, who decided to turn it into a mausoleum for his family and as a burial place for the Sforza family; in 1497 his wife Beatrice d'Este was buried there.

Between 1553 and 1778, the convent of Santa Maria delle Grazie went from being a place of worship to the seat of the Inquisition tribunal and later also a barracks. The church was almost destroyed by American bombing in 1943, the refectory was razed to the ground and only a few walls were saved, including that of the Cenacle. The Milanese, with determination and pride, rebuilt everything, handing the church back to the city in all its former glory.

The Last Supper is Leonardo da Vinci's masterpiece in the refectory of the convent of Santa Maria delle Grazie. The fresco depicts the Last Supper of Jesus with his apostles, and is alone worth a trip to Milan.

The Last Supper or Last Supper was commissioned to Leonardo by Ludovico il Moro and is based on the Gospel of John 13:21, is dated between 1495 and 1498, and depicts the moment when the Son of God announces that he will be betrayed by one of his disciples.

The work is rich in meaning, detail and symbolism, is famous and known all over the world and is one of the masterpieces of the Italian Renaissance.

Don't forget to also have a look at the fresco of the Crucifixion, on the opposite side, which completes the sense of the room's decoration. It is a work by Donato Montorfano, designed specifically to confront the Last Supper: on the one hand, Jesus pledges to offer his material body for the remission of sins, and on the other he fulfils that commitment by dying on the cross.

SAN MAURIZIO AL MONASTERO MAGGIORE (FREE!)

Corso Magenta, 15. Free entrance. Tuesday to Sunday, 9.30 am to 7.30 pm.

Another gem within walking distance of Piazzale Cadorna is the Church of San Maurizio al Monastero Maggiore. It is a stupendous-frescoed church, very evocative, recently restored. If you find it open, it is worth a visit, even a quick one. Admission is free, and you will find the volunteers of the FAI - Fondo Ambiente Italiano - on site, always ready to give you useful information.

The Church of San Maurizio al Monastero Maggiore was the most important Benedictine women's monastery in Milan for about a thousand years, from the 8th-9th century until 1798. Founded in the late Lombard age, it was enlarged and modified several times until it reached its present structure, a project by Gian Giacomo Dolcebuono, assisted by Battaggio and Amadeo and completed some fifteen years later by Cristoforo Solari.

The church is divided into two halves. One enters the 'public' part and notices a partition, beyond which is the Nuns' Choir, formerly reserved for cloistered nuns.

The interior of the church is spectacular. It contains a monumental cycle of frescoes that synthesises 16th century Lombard painting. With works by Bernardino Luini, and his sons Aurelio, Evangelista and Giovan Pietro; by Boltraffio and Simone Peterzano.

After visiting the first half, one can pass through the partition and enter the Nuns' Choir. Here we point out many wooden church furnishings and a large fresco of Noah's Ark. Curiosity: two unicorns are also painted.

THE ARCHAEOLOGICAL MUSEUM (MUSEO ARCHEOLOGICO)

Corso Magenta 15. Tuesday to Sunday, 10 am to 5.30 pm. Last admission one hour before. Full 5 euros, reduced 3 euros (university students, under25s, over65s), free for minors. This museum is included in the Abbonamento Musei Lombardia, the Milano Museum Card and the TouristMuseum Card.

Adjacent to the Church of San Maurizio is the Milan Archaeological Museum. It contains no sensational exhibits, but provides an overview of both ancient Milan, from the earliest civilisations to the Romans, and of more distant peoples, such as the Greeks, Etruscans, and even India.

The highlights of the museum, in our opinion, are:
- Roman artefacts from the Milan area, on the ground floor immediately after the entrance;
- the Diatreta Trivulzio couple;

- the Patera of Parabiago, a Roman silver ritual dish from around the 3rd-4th century, on the ground floor
- the Treasure of Lovere, a large set of silver vessels dating back to the 3rd century AD, including the beautiful Fisherman's Cup;
- an altar painted with the goddess Tellus, or perhaps the goddess Ceres, found in Milan, near the present-day Via Circo;
- the remains of ancient Caesarea Marittima;
- the Polygonal Tower from the 3rd century AD, which can be visited;
- the Gandhara Art Gallery, India, in the basement.

BASILICA SANT'AMBROGIO *(FREE)*

Piazza Sant'Ambrogio, 15. Free admission Monday to Saturday from 10 a.m. to 12.30 p.m. and 2.30 p.m. to 6 p.m. On public holidays and Sundays from 8 a.m. to 1 p.m. and 3 p.m. to 8 p.m. No sightseeing is possible during religious services.

The Basilica of Sant'Ambrogio, dedicated to the city's patron saint St. Ambrose, dates back to the 4th century AD. The first Basilica was built between 379 and 386 on the extramural necropolis of Porta Vercellina, where Christians martyred during the Roman persecutions had been buried.

In the 11th century, the Basilica di Sant'Ambrogio was rebuilt in the Lombard Romanesque style, and although it was severely damaged by Allied bombing during World War II, even with the renovation it has retained its original appearance.

It retained its original appearance even after renovation, which was necessary to repair the damage

It is an excellent example of the Romanesque style, with some characteristics specific to Lombardy.

The church is preceded by a quadriporticus, a huge atrium containing some archaeological remains. Behind it, two brick towers of different heights stand out.

The façade has some typical Lombard Romanesque elements. The 'hut' shape, made up of two overlapping loggias; the use of a poor material such as red bricks; the presence of hanging arches and pilasters.

The main entrance portal has a rich and detailed relief decoration.

Inside, we point out:

- the altar of St Ambrose, made in the 9th century by Vuolvino, with a golden antependium in relief with set stones;
- the ciborium, with four red porphyry columns and stucco high reliefs;
- the apsidal basin, with an 11th-century mosaic;
- the early Christian sacellum of San Vittore, a chapel that predates the church, which was located in the necropolis, and which has been preserved: it is a tribute to the Milanese martyr San Vittore;
- the Sarcophagus of Stilicho from the 14th century, with religious scenes in relief;
- in the crypt, the tombs of St Ambrose, St Gervasius and St Protasius, while under the pulpit is the Sarcophagus of Stilicho.

Promenade along Via Torino

From Piazza del Duomo, you can take Via Torino to head towards the Navigli area. This is a purely commercial street, but with some interesting buildings.

At number 17/19 we find the **Church of San Satiro**. It is open from Monday to Saturday, from 7.30 a.m. to 6 p.m., and on Sunday afternoons from 2 to 5.30 p.m. Admission is free, but remember that it is a place of worship and prayer.

This church, dating from the late 1400s, is famous because the artist Donato Bramante inserted a perspective play, which creates the impression of a fake presbytery behind the altar. A stratagem to compensate for the lack of space.

The peculiarity of this church is precisely the fact that there is no space at the back of the altar, but upon entering, one has the opposite impression: Donato Bramante created a fake presbytery with a stuccoed barrel vault above the high altar, which simulates a non-existent depth and thus deceives the eye by giving the idea of a space that in reality does not exist.

The decorations of the coffered dome are beautiful frescoes by Bramantino and Bergognone. Inside the church we find the painting 'Madonna and Child' on the high altar and depictions of Duke Galeazzo Maria Sforza with his wife Bona of Savoy.

In the altar of the Pieta chapel, the main one, we find the work 'Lamentation of the Dead Christ', which consists of a group of 14 life-size coloured terracotta figures, a work dating back to the 15th century and created by Agostino de' Fondutis.

The neo-Renaissance façade of the church was designed by architect Giuseppe Vandoni in 1872. Unfortunately, the original façade, designed by Amadeo following Bramante's instructions, was never realised.

The **Temple of San Sebastiano** (Via Torino 28) is another church worth a quick visit, especially for the uniqueness of its architecture. The stained-glass windows date back to the 1930s and are the work of Pietro Marussig.

THE SOUTH OF MILAN

THE BASILICA OF SAN LORENZO AND THE COLUMNS

Corso di Porta Ticinese 35. Free entrance, the Chapel of St. Aquilino has a charge, 2 euros. Open Monday to Friday from 8 a.m. to 12:30 p.m. and 3 p.m. to 6:30 p.m.; Saturday and Sunday 9 a.m. to 1 p.m. and 3 p.m. to 7 p.m.

From Largo Carrobbio, at the end of Via Torino, you can take Corso di Porta Ticinese, and arrive at the Basilica of San Lorenzo.

In front of the façade of the Basilica stand 16 columns (originally 17) from Roman times, made of white marble with Corinthian capitals: these are the remains of what must have been the central nave of a church, or the internal peristyle of a rectangular basilica. The earliest restoration of the columns dates back to 1505 and they have been taken up and restored several times since then.

The columns, in the history of Milan, have risked being torn down several times because they were considered old compared to the exponential growth of the city, but fortunately they have come down to us and survived even the bombings of the Second World War.

The basilica of San Lorenzo has an architecture consisting of a two-storey circular hall with four large exedras, set off by four columns in five rooms, and around everything there is an internal portico, both on the ground and second floors. A dome with an octagonal base dominates the entire structure.

Inside, the Chapel of St. Aquilinus (the only part of the basilica that preserves the original structure in its entirety) where you can find a copy of Leonardo's Last Supper and early Christian mosaics dating back to the 6th century.

The Colonne di San Lorenzo has become a meeting point for Milan's movida and all around there are kiosks and bars where you can have aperitifs and snacks.

CHURCH OF SANT'EUSTORGIO

Piazza Sant'Eustorgio. Free entrance to the Church. Open daily from 10 a.m. to 6 p.m. The museum of Sant'Eustorgio is open Tuesday to Sunday, 10 a.m. to 6 p.m., admission 6 euro. Combined ticket with the nearby Museo Diocesano.

Continuing along Corso di Porta Ticinese, you arrive at Piazza Sant'Eustorgio, where the church of the same name stands.

The Church of Sant'Eustorgio is famous for allegedly housing the relics of the Magi from Constantinople. This church, founded in the 4th century and rebuilt in the 19th century, is the subject of a legend.

According to tradition, it was built for a divine will. Saint Eustorgio was transporting the relics of the Magi from Constantinople and it was here that the wheels of his chariot became very heavy and no one could move them any more.

Since it was impossible to reach the basilica of Santa Tecla, his original destination, Sant'Eustorgio decided to build a new basilica on that site, outside the perimeter of what was then the city of Milan.

Unfortunately, the relics were stolen during the sacking of Milan in 1162: the troops of Emperor Frederick I of Swabia seized them and took them to Cologne Cathedral. In 1904, a small part of the relics was returned and they are now kept in the sarcophagus of the Magi inside the basilica.

Architecturally, the building was built on a suburban necropolis of which there are still archaeological traces, and is Romanesque in style with three naves with cross vaults and several chapels. The façade was designed by Giovanni Brocca between 1862 and 1865.

Next to the church, the **Museum of Sant'Eustorgio** (for a fee) allows visitors to visit the early Christian necropolis, the monumental sacristy (where there are relics and liturgical furnishings), the Solarian Chapels and the Portinari Chapel, located behind the apse of the church, among the most important elements of the Milanese Renaissance.

To enhance the church, permanent night lighting has been in place since 2011, enveloping the building in a warm, soft light. On the bell tower we find the star of light, reminiscent of the comet that guided the Three Kings to the cave where Jesus was born.

The Navigli

The Navigli is one of the hubs of Milan's movida. It is one of the city's most popular and beautiful areas both during the day - with its bookshops, vintage shops and aperitif bars - and for going out at night.

The Navigli are a set of artificial canals that were once used to transport goods and for irrigation. Through these canals, marble from the Candoglia quarries was brought to Milan and used to build the Duomo.

They can also be found in other parts of the city, but 'the Navigli' par excellence are the Naviglio Pavese and the Naviglio Grande.

The history of the Navigli began in the 12th century, these canals were intended to connect Milan to Lake Maggiore, Lake Como, the city of Pavia and the river Po, these 'Waterways' served to transport goods and materials to and from Milan and thus to make the city of Milan grow and develop.

Leonardo da Vinci also worked on the Navigli project and was commissioned to do so in the 15th century by Ludovico Il Moro. Until the 19th century, the Navigli were the main transport system, then they were gradually replaced by road transport, which was much faster and more efficient.

Over time, many of the Navigli were buried and forgotten for many years, then there was a redevelopment in the Porta Genova area and the Navigli are now used for small city cruises and are one of the most frequented places by Milanese and tourists.

In the Navigli area, you can visit the Vicolo dei Lavandai, one of the wash-houses where women have been cleaning clothes for centuries.

CHURCH OF ST. EUPHEMIA

Piazza Sant'Eufemia. Free admission. Open Monday to Saturday, 7.45 a.m. to 12 noon and 3.30 p.m. to 6.30 p.m. Sundays and public holidays 7:45 a.m. - 12 noon and 4 p.m. - 6:30 p.m.

This ancient basilica was founded around 475 but has been rebuilt and remodelled several times. The present façade dates back to the 1870s and is in Neo-Romanesque style.

The interior is neo-Gothic in style.

The main works of art:

- the Marriage of St Catherine, by the School of Leonardo, in the first chapel on the left
- Madonna and Child with Saints by Marco d'Oggiono, third chapel on the left
- the Brasca Tomb, by sculptor Cristoforo Solari (known as 'il Gobbo')
- Madonna of the Holy Rosary, painting by Augusto Lozzia.

Mudec - Museum of Cultures

56 Via Tortona. Open Tuesday, Wednesday, Friday and Sunday from 09:30 to 19:30, Monday from 14:30 to 19:30, Thursday and Saturday from 9:30 to 22:30. The visit to the permanent collection is free, the cost of temporary exhibitions is variable.

The Mudec Museo delle Culture narrates the cultures of different peoples. It hosts a permanent exhibition, which is free of charge, and temporary exhibitions, which generally charge an entrance fee, which is different for each exhibition.

The permanent collection has 7,000 works from all continents, covering a historical period from 2000 BC to the present day. These include Picasso's painting La Femme Nue.

Current exhibitions can be found on the official website.

The Mudec project was born around 1990 when the City of Milan acquired the former industrial area of the Ansaldo company: the idea was to transform former industrial poles into cultural spaces.

The design of Mudec was entrusted to the British architect David Chipperfield. The structure is divided into two floors and the entire building is based on the contrast between the curves of the central space and the geometric volumes of the various exhibition halls.

The Prada Foundation (Fondazione Prada)

Ex-distilleria Società Italiana Spiriti in Largo Isarco, 2. Open Mondays, Wednesdays, and Thursdays from 10 a.m. to 7 p.m. Fridays, Saturdays, and Sundays from 10 a.m. to 9 p.m. Full price ticket for temporary and permanent exhibitions costs 15 euros, reduced price ticket 12 euros (students under 26, FAI members), free entrance for under 18s, over 65s and disabled persons. Check at the ticket office for other reductions.

The Fondazione Prada is dedicated to contemporary art and film. It was founded by Miuccia Prada and Patrizio Bertelli in 1993.

The Fondazione Prada hosts exhibitions of various kinds, mainly by international contemporary artists. Inside the building is Bar Luce, designed by Wes Anderson to recreate the atmosphere of a typical 1950s Milanese bar.

On the sixth floor of the building is the **Ristorante Torre**, designed by Rem Koolhaas and run by chef Lorenzo Lunghi.

North East Milan: from Corso Venezia to Buenos Aires

Quadrilatero della Moda - Fashion District

The Quadrilatero della Moda (Fashion District) is one of the world's most famous luxury shopping areas with boutiques, ateliers, and showrooms of the most important Italian and international fashion brands. A true 'square' formed by four streets: via Monte

Napoleone, via Della Spiga, via Manzoni and Corso Venezia. There are also via Borgospesso, via Santo Spirito, via Gesù, via Sant'Andrea and via Bagutta, equally luxurious and well-kept, but a little less emblazoned and famous.

People from all over the world visit the Quadrilatero della Moda, either to shop or to admire the shop windows. According to the Main streets across the world index, Via Monte Napoleone is one of the most expensive and prestigious streets in the world.

In the area there are also:

- the Bagatti Valsecchi Museum, an interesting house-museum containing the collection of paintings and art artefacts from the 15th and 16th centuries collected by the Bagatti Valsecchi brothers (Via Gesù 5, full admission €15, concessions available, closed Mondays and Tuesdays, Wednesday open from 1 to 8 p.m., Thursday and Friday from 1 to 5.45 p.m., Saturday and Sunday from 10 a.m. to 5.45 p.m.)
- Palazzo Morando, which houses the Costume, Fashion, and Image Museum (Via S. Andrea 6, free entrance, open Tuesday to Sunday from 10 a.m. to 5.30 p.m., last entrance at 5 p.m.).

POLDI PEZZOLI MUSEUM

Via Alessandro Manzoni, 12, 20121 Milan Full price ticket costs 10 euro, reduced price ticket 7 euro, school ticket 3 euro. Every day from 10 am to 6 pm. The museum is closed on Tuesdays, New Year's Eve, Easter, 25 April, 1 May, 15 August, 1 November, 8 December and Christmas. Last admission is at 5.30 p.m. Included in the Abbonamento Musei Lombardia.

The Poldi Pezzoli Museum is part of the 'Case Museo di Milano' and houses the works of art donated by the Milanese collector Gian Giacomo Poldi Pezzoli (1822-1879). It is located in the centre of Milan, near La Scala Theatre.

The museum contains the works of important artists including Perugino, Piero della Francesca, Sandro Botticelli, Antonio Pollaiolo, Giovanni Bellini, Michelangelo Buonarroti, Pinturicchio, Filippo Lippi, Andrea Mantegna, Jacopo Palma il Vecchio, Francesco Hayez, Giovanni Battista Tiepolo, Jusepe de Ribera, Canaletto, Lucas Cranach il Vecchio and Luca Giordano.

The Poldi Pezzoli Museum is divided into two floors and over the years the number of works has increased thanks to numerous donations ranging from embroidery to watchmaking to painting.

Among the most important donations are Bruno Falk's collection of mechanical clocks (1973) and Piero Portaluppi's collection of sundials (donated by his daughter Luisa, 1978); in 1998, thanks to Arnaldo Pomodoro, an armoury room was set up. Since 1968, a workshop for the restoration of antique weapons and armour has also been set up in the museum.

A STROLL ALONG CORSO VENEZIA

Corso Venezia is a beautiful, albeit busy, street. As you stroll along, you will come across various mansions and palaces, ranging from the 1400s to the 1900s.

Nearby, at 14 Via Mozart, is **Villa Necchi Campiglio**, managed by the FAI Fondo Ambiente Italiano, which houses several works of art. Admission costs 12 euros, but there are reductions: students up to 26 years of age pay 5 euros.

It is open Wednesday to Sunday from 10 a.m. to 6 p.m., with last admission at 5.15 p.m. It is closed on Mondays and Tuesdays.

Villa Necchi Campiglio is the house owned by the Necchi sisters, the owners of the company that produces the famous Necchi sewing machines. The Villa is managed by the FAI and houses masterpieces by Canaletto, De Chirico and many other artists. Villa Necchi Campiglio was designed between 1932 and 1935 by architect Piero Portaluppi at the request of sisters Gigina and Nedda Necchi and Gigina's husband, Angelo Campiglio.

In the years when families were building mansions, they chose to create a single-family villa surrounded by greenery, a wonderful house with every comfort: lift, dumbwaiter, heated swimming pool (the first private pool in Milan), tennis courts, gym, and screening room.

During the war, the villa was requisitioned and became the headquarters of Alessandro Pavolini of the Republic of Salò.

When they returned to their home, the Necchi Campiglio family felt the need to make it more welcoming and turned to the architect Tomaso Buzzi, who added marble, fireplaces and special, elegant furniture. Angelo Campiglio and Gigina Necchi, together with their sister Nedda, have always lived in their villa.

Upon Campiglio's death, the two Necchi sisters decided to leave their house to FAI (the foundation of their great friend Alberto Veronesi), the handover came in 2001 with the death of the last surviving sister, Gigina.

FAI took care of the Necchi Campiglio heritage and enriched the villa with the art collections of Claudia Gian Ferrari and Alighiero dé Micheli, who embellished the walls of the villa with the works of important painters such as De Chirico, Canaletto, Sironi, Tiepolo and Martini.

Etruscan Museum - Luigi Rovati Foundation

Corso Venezia 51. Open Wednesday to Sunday from 10am to 8pm (last entrance is at 7pm). Admission costs €16, €12 for over-65s and students (with ID) under 26. Reduced price 8 euro for visitors aged between 11 and 18. Other reductions are available.

Free admission on the first Sunday of every month. This museum is not included in the Abbonamento Musei Lombardia.

Inaugurated in 2022, the Etruscan Museum of the Luigi Rovati Foundation houses a collection of 200 pieces including art and objects from the Etruscan civilisation, which developed in central Italy before the rise of Rome, with a very modern layout also from an architectural point of view.

The experience is complemented by several modern and contemporary works in the exhibition space and some temporary exhibitions, which are included in the entrance fee.

In the Pavilion in the garden there are free temporary exhibitions that can be visited.

NATURAL HISTORY MUSEUM

The Natural History Museum, Corso Venezia 55, is not of particular interest to tourists, but the building that houses it is worth a look from the outside.

PORTA VENEZIA

At the end of Corso Venezia is the imposing Porta Venezia, one of the gates that opened onto the Spanish walls of Milan. It was rebuilt in neoclassical style in the first half of the 19th century.

THE ART NOUVEAU HOUSES OF VIA MALPIGHI

A few steps from the gate is Via Malpighi, a short street with two Art Nouveau houses. They cannot be visited, but it is possible to observe their exterior façade.

At Via Malpighi 3 is Casa Galimberti, while at Via Malpighi 12 is Casa Guazzoni. There are many other Art Nouveau buildings in Milan.

A STROLL ALONG CORSO BUENOS AIRES

Corso Buenos Aires, historically one of Milan's shopping streets, starts at Porta Venezia: 1.2 kilometres long and more than 350 shops of all kinds, from fast fashion to ice cream parlours.

The street was created at the behest of Emperor Joseph II of Austria and officially came into being in 1782; the original name was Corso Loreto, due to the proximity of the shrine dedicated to Santa Maria di Loreto.

In 1906, on the occasion of the first Universal Exhibition, a name change was decreed to give an international flavour to the city and to pay homage to the first two countries that joined the event, which were Argentina and Peru, hence the birth of Piazza Lima and Piazza Argentina.

There are a few buildings worth noting and observing as you stroll along the street.

Palazzo Luraschi, Corso Buenos Aires 1, dating back to 1887, decorated with some columns from the former Lazzaretto di Milano and with medallions and busts inspired by the novel 'I promessi sposi' (The Betrothed). It was restored in 2016.

At **Corso Buenos Aires 19** a beautiful neoclassical building from the late 1700s.

At **Corso Buenos Aires 33** stands the Teatro Elfo Puccini, inaugurated in 1902 and restored in 2010, which is now the current home of the Compagnia dell'Elfo.

Palazzo Argentina (Corso Buenos Aires 36) designed by Piero Bottoni, is a classic example of Italian architecture from the second half of the 20th century. It was in fact built in 1946, immediately after the Second World War.

The **Casa Centenara** (Corso Buenos Aires 66) is an Art Nouveau building built in 1907 by architect Giovan Battista Bossi.

At Corso Buenos Aires 75, on the other hand, a 1920s building in deco style stands out, housing shops and offices.

BOSCHI DI STEFANO HOUSE MUSEUM

Via Giorgio Jan 15. Open Tuesday to Sunday, 10 a.m. - 6 p.m. Free visit.

A few steps from Corso Buenos Aires, the Casa Museo Boschi di Stefano houses a collection of 20th-century Italian art in an Art Deco-style flat, donated to the City of Milan in 1974.

The Boschi di Stefano House Museum was inaugurated on 5 February 2003 in the house once inhabited by Antonio Boschi (1896-1988) and Marieda Di Stefano (1901-1968).

Around 300 of the more than 2,000 works in their private collection can be admired.

The collection is a cross-section of 20th century Italian art history and includes paintings, sculptures, and drawings made between the first decade of the 20th century and the end of the 1960s.

MILAN NORTH WEST

PORTA NUOVA

The Porta Nuova district stretches around the Porta Garibaldi railway and metro station. It is a futuristic and modern area, a few steps away from historical areas, such as Corso Como, Corso Garibaldi and the Isola district, stretch very recent buildings that have transformed Milan's skyline.

This area has been completely redesigned in recent years by world-class architects. Some projects are still in progress. Today it is one of the most futuristic areas in Milan.

The most important buildings in the Porta Nuova Project are the skyscrapers, designed to house offices, shops and housing.

In **Piazza Gae Aulenti** are the two Towers, including the UniCredit Tower, designed by architect César Pelli, which, at 231 metres, is the tallest skyscraper in Italy to date.

A stone's throw from the square is a curious building, resembling a wicker basket: these are the IBM Studios. They cannot be visited and host events and other activities of the large American computer company.

From Piazza Gae Aulenti you can admire the two buildings of the Bosco Verticale, one of Milan's symbols. According to a survey, it is the most shared place on Instagram by tourists: a real challenge to the Duomo! These are two residential towers, decorated with planted terraces, designed by architect Stefano Boeri as 'green skyscrapers', i.e. eco-sustainable and self-sufficient. A model that has become a source of inspiration for other projects around the world.

Continuing towards Viale della Liberazione, one glimpses the Aria and Solaria Towers, two residential buildings by Studio Acquitectonic. A little further on, the Torre Diamante, which currently houses the Milan offices of the BNP Paribas Group.

Corso Como

Just a few minutes' walk from Piazza Gae Aulenti and Porta Garibaldi station is Corso Como, a pedestrian and commercial street just 280 metres long. After the Second World War, this street was the focus of a project of the Milan City Council, which wanted to build offices and luxury housing. The project only partly materialised (although, a few decades later, the nearby Piazza Gae Aulenti took off) and Corso Como was sidelined for a long time.

In the 1990s it became the centre of the so-called 'Milano da bere', that of carefree nightlife. With the Porta Nuova project, Corso Como became a pedestrian street with luxury shops, bars, and restaurants of all kinds.

At night, as in many nightlife areas, it is advisable to watch out for pickpockets.

The Isola District

A stone's throw from Porta Nuova, the Isola district is today one of the most popular areas of the city, with a very intense nightlife. This district developed in the late 1800s and owes its name to the fact that the railway network physically isolated it from the rest of the city, making it an 'Island' within the tracks.

Isolation has allowed the neighbourhood to develop differently and to develop its own identity, almost as if it were a village apart, calm and far away from the chaos of the city.

Since the 1980s, this district has become trendy, with special design and handicraft shops, but also many restaurants and aperitif bars, which to this day continue to be a favourite among the Milanese and tourists.

There are no particular monuments on Isola, but architecture lovers can appreciate Casa Ghiringhelli (Piazzale Lagosta 2) and Casa Comolli Rustici (Via Guglielmo Pepe 32) built by architects Terragni and Lingeri in the rationalist style in the 1930s.

But, more generally, Isola is a good area to relax and go out for dinner or a drink.

VIA PAOLO SARPI - CHINATOWN

Also in the west of the city, Via Paolo Sarpi is Milan's 'Chinatown'. It is now a pedestrianised street and very crowded, especially at weekends.

Since the beginning of the 20th century, this area of Milan has attracted many Chinese immigrants, who over the years have created a community within the city. From Via Paolo Sarpi branch off small streets and side streets that host all kinds of Chinese businesses.

Besides shopping, the Milanese (and tourists) also appreciate the restaurants and the many street food shops. There is no shortage, however, of historic businesses, some run by Italians, especially bars and wine bars. Among the prominent establishments:

- the Sarpi ravioleria for Chinese dumplings;
- the Cantine Isola, a historic wine shop on the street;

- butcher's shop Sirtori, a historic Milanese shop taken over a few years ago by a Chinese entrepreneur;
- OTTO, a western-style club specialising in gin for aperitifs or after-dinner drinks.

THE MONUMENTAL CEMETERY *(FREE)*

Piazzale Cimitero Monumentale, MM5 Monumentale stop. Admission is free and the cemetery is open from Tuesday to Sunday, 9.30 am to 5 pm.

The monumental cemetery is the cemetery where people who have brought prestige to the city of Milan are buried. It was established in 1866 as a cemetery open to all Milanese 'in all forms and all fortunes'.

It was designed by architect Carlo Maciachini and covers an area of 250,000 square metres in which we find Gothic, Lombard Romanesque, Pisan and Byzantine influences, a place of worship and beauty also called an 'open-air museum'.

It is divided into three areas. In the centre are the Catholic dead, on the right the non-Catholic dead, and on the left the 'Departure of the Israelites'. Very significant is the Famedio, i.e. 'the temple of fame', in which the most illustrious people are buried and in which the names of people buried elsewhere, but who made an important contribution to the history of the city, are engraved.

On 2 November each year, new names are added.

At the entrance there is an Info Point, set up in 2013, where you can ask for a map of the cemetery where the most famous graves are marked: the cemetery is very large and without a map you risk wandering around for hours.

Guided tours, lasting one and a half hours, are also organised.

Corso Sempione

Corso Sempione crosses the city in a north-westerly direction. It starts at the Arco della Pace and continues to Piazza Firenze.

It is a tree-lined, predominantly residential avenue, which is entirely practicable by bicycle thanks to two recently created cycle paths.

Some noteworthy buildings:

- at Corso Sempione 25, the headquarters of a fascist district group built in the late 1930s in the style of the period;
- the RAI headquarters at Corso Sempione 27, built in 1939 to a design by architect Gio Ponti;
- the Vespa skyscraper, built in 1955, at 43 Corso Sempione;
- Casa Rustici, Corso Sempione 36, in rationalist style, built in the 1930s to a design by Pietro Lingeri and Giuseppe Terragni.

City Life district

Close to Corso Sempione is City Life (MM5 stop Tre Torri), another recently built area. It is a redevelopment project in an area where the buildings of an old trade fair used to stand.

City Life consists of two squares called Piazza Alberto Burri and Piazza Tre Torri. The latter square is named after three skyscrapers used as offices.

Isozaki Tower, owned by Arata Isozaki and spanning 207 metres by 50 storeys and nicknamed 'The Straight'.

The **Hadid Tower**, owned by Generali, designed by Zaha Hadid and inspired by an imaginary sail shaken by the wind, hence the nickname 'The Crooked': it stretches 175 metres by 40 storeys.

Libeskind Tower, designed by Daniel Libeskind and nicknamed 'The Curved' because of its shape inspired by a sphere enveloping the square. It is 160 metres high and houses the offices of PwC.

Surrounding the Three Towers is a newly created park, which is very popular, especially at weekends.

The City Life shopping centre offers all kinds of shops and a food court with Italian and international food.

SAN SIRO STADIUM

San Siro is easily accessible by public transport, with stops at the MM5 San Siro Ippodromo and San Siro Stadio. For those arriving by car, several car parks are available nearby. Guided tours including the Stadium Museum can be booked on the website www.sansirostadium.com/museum-tour/

The history of San Siro began in 1925, when Piero Pirelli, president of AC Milan, decided to build a stadium next to the city's hippodrome. The inauguration took place on 19 September 1926 with a derby between Inter and Milan, won 6-3 by the

Nerazzurri. Initially, the stadium was home only to AC Milan, but in 1947 Inter also became co-owners. In 1980, the stadium was named after Giuseppe Meazza, a famous footballer who played for both AC Milan and Inter.

The San Siro Stadium tour offers a unique experience for football fans. During the tour, it is possible to visit the dressing rooms, the press room and the pitch. Visitors can also access the museum, which houses an extensive collection of historical memorabilia of the two Milanese teams. The tour is an unmissable opportunity to immerse yourself in the history of Milanese football.

San Siro is not only a football stadium, but also a venue for concerts and other events. Besides Milan and Inter Milan matches, the stadium has hosted European cup finals and matches of the 1990 World Cup. Its capacity of 80,018 makes it one of the largest stadiums in Europe. The first citizen continues to support the idea of renovating and selling the Meazza to the two Milanese teams.

The Certosa (Charterhouse) of Garegnano

Via Garegnano 28. It is open from Monday to Saturday, from 9:30 a.m. to 12 noon and from 3:30 p.m. to 5:15 p.m. Free admission. A bit far from the city centre, in a residential area. Tourists are rare.

In the suburban area, reachable by tram 14 in the direction of Cimitero Maggiore (you can take this tram from Via Torino, near the Duomo, or at the MM5 stop Cenisio, the last metro stop touched by the tram route). Calculate a walk of about ten minutes from the tram stop: we suggest you get help from Google Maps or another navigator.

In the centre of a residential area stands the Certosa di Garegnano, founded in 1349 by Bishop Giovanni Visconti. Inside, it is decorated with splendid frescoes by Daniele Crespi, Bernardo Zenale and Simone Peterzano, who went down in history as the master of Caravaggio.

The Charterhouse risked coming to a bad end because, for years, it was given in pieces to various owners who used it as residences for the farmers who tended the surrounding land. Thanks to the intervention of Don Filippo Premoli, the parish priest of the village of Garegnano, the Charterhouse was returned to the Church. In 1783, the parish of Garegnano was installed in the monastery premises and became Santa Maria Assunta in Certosa. Illustrious figures such as Petrarch, St Bernardine of Siena, Philip IV of Spain and Lord Byron have passed through the Certosa di Milano.

It is a place of worship and prayer still used by the Milanese and definitely off the traditional tourist track.

Milan North

Stazione Centrale - Central Station

Milan's Stazione Centrale (Piazza Duca d'Aosta, 1) is the city's main railway station. It was inaugurated in 1931 and is an architectural masterpiece that mixes neoclassicism, libery and art deco, with a strong imprint from the fascist regime that had been ruling Italy for several years at the time.

The façade is monumental and two enormous winged horses stand out on a terrace. All the rooms, including the interior (which is very crowded) are inspired by the monuments of the Roman Empire. The interior rooms are decorated with various motifs and statues, some in plaster, others in concrete.

On rare occasions, it is possible to visit the Royal Pavilion, an area of the station that was reserved for the Italian royal family and its court, with rich marble decoration. Unfortunately, it is only open to the public when hosting exhibitions or on special occasions.

Inside the station is the Holocaust Memorial, near an old platform, number 21, from which trains departed to take Jewish deportees to the Nazi death camps.

THE PIRELLONE

In front of the Central Station stands the Pirelli Skyscraper, nicknamed the Pirellone. Designed by a team of architects, including Gio Ponti, it was completed in 1961 and for decades was the seat of the Lombardy Region, as well as being the highest point in Milan. In 2022 it was hit by a small tourist plane, an event still vivid in the memory of many Milanese.

PALAZZO LOMBARDIA AND ITS TERRACE

Palazzo Lombardia (Piazza Città di Lombardia), also called Palazzo della Regione, was built by Pei Cobb Freed & Partners of New York, Caputo Partnership and Sistema Duemila and was inaugurated 21 March 2011, on the 150th anniversary of the Unification of Italy.

At 161 metres high, Palazzo Lombardia is the city's tallest skyscraper. After 50 years of undisputed supremacy, the Pirellone had to yield the sceptre to Milan's new skyline.

The palace can be visited exceptionally on a few Sundays a year, free of charge. The 'Belvedere Experience' allows you to go up to the 39th floor. Animals are not allowed. Booking is compulsory from the page https://eventi.regione.lombardia.it/esplora-eventi, which also presents other events taking place in the palace, usually for a fee.

On the ground floor of the building is IsolaSET, a space dedicated to temporary art exhibitions.

HANGAR BICOCCA (FREE)

Via Chiese, 2. Open Thursday to Sunday, 10am-10pm. Closed Mondays, Tuesdays and Wednesdays. Last admission to the exhibitions is at 9.15 pm. Free admission.

Hangar Bicocca is an exhibition space dedicated to the promotion of contemporary art. It covers an area of 15,000 square metres and is located in the Bicocca industrial district, north of the city. You can get there with the MM1 (Sesto Marelli) or MM5 (Ponale) metro lines and then take a bus (51 or 87) or bike share, or opt for a walk.

The name comes from the Bicocca degli Arcimboldi, a historic country villa from the 15th century that can still be visited today.

Hangar Bicocca is a classic example of industrial archaeology, these spaces were obtained from the conversion of the former Breda factory, a company founded in 1886 where steam and electric locomotives were built.

It hosts temporary exhibitions and some permanent exhibitions, including:

- Fausto Melotti's 'La Sequenza' sculptures
- Anselm Kiefer's installation 'The Seven Heavenly Palaces'.

Milan... for enthusiasts

If you love ancient history: Roman Milan

Milan, known as Mediolanum during the Roman Empire, was a city of great strategic and cultural importance. Its geographical position and advanced infrastructure made it a vital centre for trade, politics and daily life. In this article we will explore various aspects of Roman Milan, from its urban structures to its communication routes, from daily life to its function as the capital of the Western Roman Empire.

The first walls of Mediolanum date back to Republican times, probably built under the principate of Octavian Augustus. The city gates, such as Porta Romana and Porta Ticinese, were essential for the defence and control of access to the city. Today's historic city centre traces the area of ancient Mediolanum, remains of which can still be seen.

The forum of Mediolanum was the beating heart of public and political life. It was home to important buildings such as the basilica, theatre, and circus. The forum was a meeting and exchange place, where the main commercial and social activities took place.

The private dwellings in Mediolanum, known as domus, were often richly decorated with mosaics and frescoes. Some remains of these dwellings have been found in the modern Via Gorani and Piazza Borromeo. The domus were equipped with porticoed courtyards and heated rooms, demonstrating a high level of comfort and luxury for the time.

Milan as Capital of the Western Roman Empire

In 286 A.D., Emperor Diocletian decided to divide the Roman Empire into two parts, entrusting the western portion to Maximian. Milan, then known as Mediolanum, was chosen as the capital of the Western Roman Empire. This decision marked the beginning of a period of great splendour for the city, which became an important political and economic centre.

The choice of Mediolanum as capital was part of the administrative reorganisation of the empire known as the tetrarchy. Diocletian and Maximian, together with their deputies, ruled from different cities to better control the vast territories. Mediolanum, thanks to its strategic location and infrastructure, became the beating heart of the Roman West.

The Imperial Palace

Maximian embellished Mediolanum with numerous monuments, including the grandiose imperial palace on today's Via Brisa. This complex included residences, private baths and places of worship. The palace was directly connected to the Roman circus, allowing the emperor access to it without going out into the street. This imperial quarter represented the centre of power and political life in the city.

The Edict of Milan

In 313 A.D., Emperor Constantine promulgated the Edict of Milan, a fundamental document that guaranteed religious freedom in the empire. This event marked a crucial moment in the history of Mediolanum, further consolidating its role as capital and centre of political and social innovation. Mediolanum maintained its status as capital until 402 AD, when the imperial court was transferred to Ravenna for strategic reasons.

Hydraulic Works and Infrastructure

During Roman times, Milan saw the construction of numerous **hydraulic works**. Among these, the diversion of rivers was crucial to ensure an adequate water supply for the city. The ancient Romans altered the course of rivers and streams to bring additional water to Mediolanum, thus meeting the growing needs of the population and greatly improving the quality of life.

The **Vetra Canal**, created by the ancient Romans, was an important hydraulic infrastructure. This canal collected water from the Olona river and channelled it towards the moat of the Roman walls of Milan. Its construction allowed for better management of the city's water resources, making it possible to irrigate and supply water for various public and private uses.

Unlike other Roman cities, **Mediolanum did not require large aqueducts**, as water was abundant and easily accessible thanks to nearby springs and streams. However, Roman baths were a key element of daily life, offering not only a place for physical well-being but also for socialising. Roman waterworks, therefore, not only satisfied practical needs, but also contributed to the social cohesion of the community.

The tour of roman Milan

We start in **Via San Giovanni sul Muro**: here you find traces of the ancient circle of walls and above all Porta Vercellina (49 BC), on the corner with Via Meravigli. You are on the border of the Roman walls. Please note: the name 'Porta Vercellina' was later used for three other gates that gave access to the city in the later city walls.

This one in via San Giovanni sul Muro is the original one.

Then go to **Brisa Street** to see the few remains of Emperor Maximian's palace (AD 250-310).

Maximian had an ancient hippodrome built, one of the two towers of which can be seen, which has been transformed into the bell tower of the convent of San Maurizio Maggiore. There is also an octagonal mausoleum, contained in a sarcophagus that has now become a baptismal font, which can be found in the Milan Cathedral. Along Via Brisa we also encounter the remains of the Roman Baths.

Now continue walking to **Piazza Affari** and then head towards **Via San Vittore al Teatro**: you will come across the remains of an ancient theatre, the city's oldest public building dating back to the 1st century BC.

Pop into Via Morigi 2: you can admire the remains of a mortar floor with marble inserts that were part of a domus.

Keep walking: between **Via Circo and Via Vigna** stood the circus built at the end of the 3rd century A.D. by Emperor Maximianus Herculeus and later demolished in 1162 A.D. by Barbarossa or the Milanese themselves. You have to imagine, though: there is no trace of the monument, only the street name remains.

Go now to **Largo Carrobbio** to admire **the Torre dei Musulmani**, the only surviving remnant of the Porta Ticinensis (Ticinese Gate) from the 1st century BC. You can also see traces of the foundation slab, which can be visited through the basement, of the octagonal body of the Chapel of Sant'Aquilino that belonged to a public building dating back to the end of the 1st century AD.

You have arrived in the area of Corso di Porta Ticinese where there are the **Colonne di San Lorenzo**, a marble colonnade in front of the façade of the church of San Lorenzo: these Colonne are the best preserved Roman monument in Milan. Probably also the most famous.

Now head back towards the centre and go to via **De Amicis 13** to see the remains of the Amphitheatre, one of the largest in northern Italy, which dates back to the 1st century AD outside the city walls, in the Porta Ticinensis area. The amphitheatre is open from Tuesday to Saturday from 9.30 to 16.30: the visit is free.

Continue to **Piazza San Sepolcro** where the Roman Forum used to be: again, nothing is left, but you can admire part of the original paving in the basement of the **Pinacoteca Ambrosiana** in Milan (admission fee).

With a bit of luck, you can try going to **Largo Corsia dei Servi** where the remains of the Roman Baths are: they can be visited by entering the Chamber of Commerce (during opening hours and asking at the entrance), thanks to a specially made glass walkway. You will walk above the Baths and be able to see the remains from above.

If you have some time to spare and want to learn more about the Roman history of Milan, go to **Corso Magenta 15** to the Archaeological Museum. In the garden there are the remains of the circus and a **tower** that has been converted into a bell tower. In the museum, there is a section dedicated to the Roman period on the ground floor.

While you are at it, take a step back in time and visit the church of San Maurizio al Monastero: it is not Roman, but it is beautiful.

If you love modern history: the 20th century in Milan

Milan has been a protagonist in many phases of Italian history. It was the capital of the Roman Empire for more than 100 years, as we recount best in the Tour of Roman Milan.

In the Middle Ages and the Modern Era, it was the capital of the Duchy of Milan, saw battles and armies, and was conquered and reconquered several times. In the Lombardy-Venetia Kingdom, Milan became a bourgeois, industrious and productive city.

But it was perhaps in the 20th century that Milan became an absolute protagonist in terms of business, culture and politics.

This tour of twentieth-century Milan offers you a series of places and insights into history. You can do it on foot or use the metro. We will also suggest some museums to delve into artistic currents in particular: consider them optional, of course.

We have chosen to focus on the part of the 20th century between the early post-war period and the 1960s. The crisis, the rise of fascism and the economic boom, in short. We will follow a geographical criterion, not a historical one: in other words, we will take a long walk and explain the places we encounter, we will not precede in chronological order.

Use this tour as you see fit: explore according to your curiosity and write to our editorial team info@3giorniamilano.it if you have any suggestions.

Piazza Velasca

We start with the Velasca Tower, also the star of our Tour of the Vertical Milan. Built in the 1950s, it was immediately the subject of heated debate whether it was ugly or not. Certainly, its architecture is unique and well represents the Italian attempt to find new stylistic paths after World War II.

Palazzo di Giustizia (Tribunal)

From Piazza Velasca we take Via Larga, one of the busiest streets in the centre of Milan, and head for the **Palazzo di Giustizia**: built in 1932, it is an architectural example of 'simplified neoclassicism'. Italians born before the 1980s will remember it for the live television broadcasts during the Mani Pulite (Clean Hands) investigation, which shook Italian politics in the early 1990s and marked the transition from the First to the Second Republic.

Off the beaten track, along the way you will pass the **Sanctuary of San Bernardino alle Ossa**: it is well worth taking a break to visit. It takes its name from the Ossuary, a room entirely decorated with skulls or bones.

The Duomo Cathedral area

Head back towards the centre, setting the Duomo as your destination on Google Maps. On the way you will probably pass by Piazza Fontana. Here you will find a bank branch, where the **terrible 1969 bombing** took place in which 17 people lost their lives. This event is considered by some historians to be the beginning of the 'Anni di Piombo'.

Continue towards Piazza del Duomo. Right next to the left side of the city cathedral is **La Rinascente**, Milan's cult shopping centre, housed in a building rebuilt after a fire and opened in 1921. It is not only a shopping venue, but the symbol of Milan's fashion industry, as well as a splendid example of the architecture of the time.

To the right of the Duomo is the Palazzo dell'Arengario. Built between 1937 and 1956, it was the last building in the urban renewal project for the centre of Milan, which also included the redevelopment of the nearby Piazza Diaz.

You can peek into the Piazza to see some buildings from that period. Then head back to the Palazzo dell'Arengario. Here you will find the **Museo del Novecento**, the first artistic stop on our tour.

In this museum, you will find many works from the Italian 20th century period, including the artistic avant-gardes. The most famous is Futurism.

Palazzo Mezzanotte

When you are ready to move on, set your destination as Palazzo Mezzanotte, headquarters of the Italian Stock Exchange.

Google Maps will probably take you past **Piazza San Sepolcro** (this square is also on the tour of Roman Milan). It was here that **Mussolini** founded the Fasci Italiani di Combattimento in 1919: you are therefore in the **birthplace of Fascism**.

Continue on to Piazza Affari. In front of you is Palazzo Mezzanotte, named after the architect Paolo

Mezzanotte, who designed it and directed its construction. The building's façade is a perfect example of 20th-century style in architecture.

In front of the Stock Exchange is the obviously later sculpture L.O.V.E. by Maurizio Cattelan. The interpretation of the work leaves little doubt. The fact that it faces the headquarters of the Stock Exchange, then, is definitely indicative.

Nearby, you will find many impressive buildings from the 20th century period. Take a stroll to browse around. When you're ready, walk or take the metro to the Porta Venezia MM1 Red Line stop.

Porta Venezia

We start from here to visit some places that tell a good story of 20th-century Milan.

The first stop is at Via Malpighi 3: Casa Galimberti. This is an Art Nouveau building: it cannot be visited inside, but the façade is worth the visit. The Art Nouveau style was very popular in the early decades of the 20th century and gave Milan several beautiful buildings. Take a few more steps and, at number 12 Via Malpighi, you will find Casa Guazzoni, another example of an Art Nouveau façade.

Boschi di Stefano House Museum

Continue on to the **Boschi Di Stefano House Museum**: which can be visited free of charge and houses an amazing collection of paintings from the 1910s to the 1960s, with period furniture.

Allow at least 30/45 minutes for a non-superficial visit. The House Museum is run by volunteers from the Italian Touring Club. Ask them to tell you some anecdotes about the history of the house and its former owners.

Loreto Square

Go ahead and walk down Corso Buenos Aires to Piazzale Loreto. You find yourself in a square full of traffic, objectively chaotic, not particularly beautiful and without tourist attractions. But there is a piece of history: **the body of Benito Mussolini was displayed here in 1945**, after his execution. Photos from that day show the corpse horribly exposed to the crowd near a petrol station, which is no longer there today. However, a journalistic reconstruction by the website Linkiesta has pinpointed the exact spot where Mussolini's body was hung. And it is where you see McDonald's today.

We are ready to move on.

The Central Station

Arriving at the Central Station forecourt, you see two symbols of Milan's 20th century.

The Central Station is an example of monumental architecture from the Fascist period.

The Pirelli skyscraper, known as the Pirellone, is instead one of the symbols of Milan's economic boom and reconstruction after World War II.

IF YOU LOVE HORROR: THE MOST MACABRE PLACES IN MILAN

The Monumental Cemetery: Between Art and the Macabre

Milan's Monumental Cemetery is a veritable open-air museum. Inaugurated on 2 November 1866, it was designed by architect Carlo Maciachini. This place is not just a cemetery, but a journey through history and art, with tombs and monuments telling fascinating and sometimes disturbing stories.

San Bernardino alle Ossa: the church of skulls

In Milan, a short distance from Piazza Duomo, stands San Bernardino alle Ossa, a church that will leave you speechless. This place is famous for its walls entirely covered in human bones, creating a unique and eerie atmosphere. If you are a fan of the macabre, this is the place for you.

The Veiled Lady of Sempione Park

Milan is not only fashion and culture, it also harbours chilling urban legends. One of the most famous is that of the Veiled Lady, a ghost said to haunt Parco Sempione since the late 19th century. The legend tells of a beautiful woman, covered by a long black veil, who appears on cold foggy nights. Her perfume of violets attracts unwary young men, who are led to a mysterious palace on the edge of the park. Here, the Veiled Lady reveals her true face: a macabre skull.

Parco Sempione, located behind the Castello Sforzesco, is where these disturbing sightings take place. Many claim to have seen the Veiled Lady on the corner of Via Paleocapa. Some say they managed to escape, but never found the mysterious building again. Others, however, went mad after the encounter. The legend lives on, fuelled by the tales of those who swear they have seen the ghost.

The palace to which the Veiled Lady leads her victims is shrouded in mystery. No one knows exactly where it is, and those who managed to escape have never been able to find it. This building, hidden among the trees in the park, has become part of the legend. Some believe that the palace only appears to those destined to meet the Veiled Lady, making the story even more fascinating and frightening.

The Devil's Column: mysteries and legends

Right in front of the Church of Sant'Ambrogio is a monument known as the 'Devil's Column'. According to legend, Saint Ambrose had a confrontation with the devil himself. During the fight, the saint hurled the devil against the column, leaving two holes that can still be seen today. It is said that in winter the smell of sulphur escapes from these holes, an ominous sign of the presence of the evil one.

The two **holes on the column** are the result of the devil's horns getting stuck during the fight with Saint Ambrose. Tradition has it that sticking one's fingers into these holes purifies one from any evil eye and curses. Moreover, on certain cold days, a faint smell of sulphur can be perceived coming from the holes, making the atmosphere even more mysterious.

Inside the **Basilica of St Ambrose**, one can find other enigmatic symbols. For example, there are two columns, one with a cross and the other with a bronze serpent, the symbol of Knowledge. This serpent is said to have been forged by Moses. These details add another layer of mystery to a place already laden with legends and disturbing stories.

Villa Triste: the dark side of the Resistance

Villa Fossati, today known as Villa Triste, is located on **Via Paolo Uccello**. During the Republic of Salò, this villa was turned into a place of torture and ill-treatment by the Koch gang, a special department of the republican police. The prisoners' screams of pain echoed down the street, making the atmosphere even more chilling.

In the dungeons of Villa Triste, partisans and anti-fascists were subjected to unspeakable torture. The Koch gang, led by Pietro Koch, used brutal methods to extort information and punish those who opposed the regime. This place became one of the most macabre symbols of the resistance in Milan.

After the end of the war, the Fossati family decided to stop living in the villa and donated it to the Immaculate Sisters of Our Lady of Sorrows. Today, **Villa Triste is run by the nuns**, but its dark history remains etched in the collective memory of the town.

Stretta Bagnera: the first Italian serial killer

In the heart of Milan, hidden among the streets of the centre, lies Stretta Bagnera, the narrowest street in the city. This alley is infamous for being the scene of the crimes of **Antonio Boggia**, Italy's first serial killer. Boggia, seemingly an ordinary man, hid a dark side that led him to commit brutal murders.

In 1851, a man presented himself to the carabinieri claiming to have escaped an attempted murder by

Boggia. This event led to the discovery of a series of murders. Boggia lured his victims into the cellar of his house in Via Bagnera, where he killed and walled them in. The bodies of four people were found hidden in the cellar, dismembered and walled up. His modus operandi was always the same: he would approach his victims, hit them with an axe and then hide them.

Today, walking through the Stretta Bagnera, one can still feel an eerie atmosphere. The walls seem to tell tales of terror and, despite the time that has passed, the alley retains an aura of mystery. If you are in Milan and want to feel a chill down your spine, a visit to this alley is a must. But beware, the walls might whisper scary stories!

The flat in Via San Gregorio 40: a family massacre

On 30 November 1946, in a flat at 40 Via San Gregorio, one of the most horrendous crimes in Milan's history took place. A woman and her three children, aged 7, 5 years and a 10-month-old infant, were found brutally murdered with bars. The city, still shaken by the war, was shocked by this tragedy.

The investigation quickly led to the arrest of Caterina Fort, known as Rina. She was the lover of Pippo Ricciardi, the murdered woman's husband and father of the three children. Rina worked as a saleswoman in Ricciardi's shop and, according to the investigators, had acted out of jealousy and revenge. Two other small corpses, Ricciardi's other children, were found in the flat. A massacre that left an indelible mark on the collective memory.

Today, the flat at 40 Via San Gregorio is still there, but the atmosphere surrounding it is charged with a palpable disquiet. Those who pass in front of that door cannot help but feel a chill down their spine, as if the walls themselves were a reminder of the terrible massacre that took place inside them. The history of this place lives on in urban tales and legends, keeping alive the memory of an event that Milan can never forget.

If you love architecture: the Skyscraper Tour

In the last twenty years, Milan has seen some very interesting buildings from an architectural point of view. We have devised a walking tour of the city, lasting about two to three hours, for architecture enthusiasts or those who want to keep their noses to the ground.

There are no entrance fees or tours inside the buildings. You can do part of the route on the metro if you are tired, or it is too hot to walk. And, of course, you can walk the stages in the order you prefer.

Piazza Velasca (MM Missori stop, yellow line 3)

Above you will see the Torre Velasca, one of the most talked-about buildings in the centre of Milan. Beautiful or ugly? You decide.

Built in the 1950s, it was immediately the subject of heated debate whether it was ugly or not. Certainly, its architecture is unique and well represents the Italian attempt to find new stylistic paths after World War II.

This building caused much controversy at the time of its construction. But today it has become an integral part of the Milanese 'panorama'.

From here take Via Larga, in front of you, and then turn into Via Rastrelli: you will find yourself after a short walk (and turning into Via Pecorari) behind the Royal Palace. Cross its courtyard to find yourself in Piazza Duomo.

The Duomo of Milan

It may seem trivial to stop here, but historically and traditionally this place is important. Above the Duomo, in fact, you see a statue of the Madonna, called 'la Madonnina' by the Milanese. Traditionally, no building in Milan can be taller than the Madonnina, i.e. more than 108.5 metres. In the 1930s, this tradition was turned into a real law: the construction sites of the Torre Velasca (which you saw earlier) and Giò Ponti's Torre Branca were prevented from exceeding this height.

In the following decades, the law was abolished, but the tradition was strong in the city's culture. How to respect it without halting the urban development and progress of the city? The solution was to bring a copy of the statue to the top of the building that, as time passed, became the tallest in Milan. Thus, the Madonnina would continue to tower over everything.

The copy was first installed at the Pirelli skyscraper (known as 'Pirellone'), then at Palazzo Lombardia (161 metres high) and, since 22 November 2015, at the Isozaki Tower, 209.2 metres high.

Don't panic: these three palaces are the next destinations on our tour.

The Pirelli Skyscraper

If you want to walk from the Duomo to the Pirellone, you can follow the directions on Google Maps or similar apps. You will have a nice walk in the centre, probably crossing Via Manzoni, walking along the Indro Montanelli Public Gardens and crossing the entire Piazza della Repubblica.

If you prefer to take the metro, go to the Duomo station of the MM3 Yellow and take a train towards

Comasina. Watch out for pickpockets, of course. You have to get off at Centrale.

You will find yourself in a square: if the Central Station is behind you, the Pirelli Skyscraper is in front of you, on the right.

Designed by a team of architects, including Gio Ponti (who also directed the work), the Pirellone was completed in 1961. For years this building was the seat of the Lombardy Region (today it houses the Regional Council) and the highest point in all of Milan.

In 2002 he was hit by a small tourist plane: an event that many Milanese people remember very well.

While you're at it, have a look at the architecture of the Central Station. We'll talk about it in our tour of 20th-century Milan. When you're ready, let's go to the next stop.

Palazzo Lombardia

We continue on foot, it only takes a few minutes. It will be hard to miss the headquarters of the Regional Administration. Set Piazza Città di Lombardia as your destination.

Take a few minutes to walk in the open space between the two buildings, covered by a glass wall. If you're lucky, you'll find a local produce market there, or a cheese or wine tasting. Great for a break.

The Giardino Verticale

Leave Piazza Città di Lombardia, take Via Restelli and turn left. Then enter via Gaetano de Castilla. You are in the Isola district, and in front of you rise the most photographed residential buildings in Milan. The Bosco Verticale.

These are private dwellings, which cannot be visited and are very exclusive. Their unique feature is the presence of many plants, hence the name. The balance between building and vegetation is perfect and is so delicate that the inhabitants do not take care of the upkeep of the greenery, which is carried out by the building administration instead.

Piazza Gae Aulenti

A few steps and you will be on Via Gae Aulenti, passing by the Passeggiata Luigi Veronelli and enjoying the surrounding park.

This 'new square' in Milan is home to tall modern buildings, with the UniCredit bank headquarters soaring with its spire, always illuminated at night. You can see it change colour, to celebrate special events or occasions.

The advice is to explore the pedestrian area around the square a bit. Take the Gioia footbridge towards Alvar Aalto Square to find a number of modern buildings, headquarters of large companies, and luxury homes.

These include the IBM Studios, reminiscent of a large wicker basket; the Solaria Tower, a tall building of exclusive housing; the Diamond Tower (housing the offices of BNP Paribas).

When you have seen everything, we are ready for the next stage.

City Life

The City Life district has been built over the last 15 years and houses, just like the Piazza Gae Aulenti area, both offices of large companies and prestigious homes.

We can walk there in about 30 minutes. Or by metro. A few minutes' walk away is the Monumental Cemetery, if you fancy a visit to an alternative location, from which you can take the MM5 Lilla metro line to City Life.

Otherwise, next to Piazza Gae Aulenti is Porta Garibaldi Station, where the MM5 Lilla stops.

In all cases, the destination is Piazza Tre Torri, Tre Torri stop of the MM5.

City Life stands in a park and is home to three skyscrapers, including the Isozaki Tower which is now the highest point in Milan. As you walk through the park, you will also notice some luxury residences, inaugurated in recent years.

If you feel like shopping, there is a modern shopping centre with all kinds of shops and several options for a snack, lunch, or dinner.

If you love football: *Milan and Inter Tour*

Milan is a unique city for football fans. It is home to two of the world's most famous teams: Milan AC and Inter FC. Besides the exciting matches, fans can explore official shops, fascinating museums and historic venues.

This article will guide you through the must-see places for every true fan.

AC Milan Store in the city centre

The AC Milan Store in Via Dante is a reference point for all Rossoneri fans. Located in the heart of Milan, it offers a wide range of official AC Milan products. It is the ideal place to find shirts, scarves and other collector's items. The shop is easily accessible and is a must for fans visiting the city.

Inter Store in the centre of Milan

Inter Store Milano, located in Galleria Passarella 2, is a paradise for Nerazzurri fans. Here you can find all official Inter FC products, from jerseys to gadgets.

The shop is closed on the days of sporting events and events organised at the San Siro stadium, so it is always best to check the opening hours before visiting.

AC Milan Store at San Siro

The AC Milan Store San Siro is located inside the famous San Siro stadium. This shop offers a wide selection of official AC Milan merchandise, perfect for fans who want to take home a piece of their favourite team. The shop is closed on the days of sporting events organised at the stadium.

Inter Store at San Siro

The Inter Store San Siro is the perfect place for Inter FC fans visiting the stadium. Here you can buy all the team's official products, from jerseys to gadgets. Like the AC Milan Store, this shop is also closed on the days of sporting events organised at the stadium.

The Mondo Milan Museum and Casa Milan

The Mondo Milan Museum offers a unique experience for all true Rossoneri fans: it is located inside Casa Milan, at 8 Via Aldo Rossi, Portello Fiera area.

The Mondo Milan Museum is open daily from 10 a.m. to 7 p.m., with the last entrance at 6 p.m. Tickets can be purchased online or at the Casa Milan ticket office. Prices vary depending on the type of ticket and any available conventions. For more information, please visit the museum's official website.

Permanent exhibitions tell the glorious history of AC Milan through trophies, historical jerseys and unforgettable memorabilia. Every corner of the museum exudes Rossoneri passion and pride.

In addition to the permanent exhibitions, the museum hosts temporary exhibitions that vary throughout the year. These exhibitions offer an in-depth look at specific moments in the club's history or particular topics related to football and sports culture.

For those who want a more in-depth experience, guided tours are available. Experienced guides lead visitors through the museum, providing details and anecdotes that enrich the visit. To reserve an exclusive guided tour, please write to mondomilan@acmilan.com.

Casa Milan is the symbol of Milan AC, located in the north-west of Milan, in the Fiera Milano City/Portello area. This modern and innovative building represents the history and tradition of the Rossoneri club. The structure is a landmark for all fans, with its unique and eye-catching design.

Casa Milan offers a wide range of services for fans. Here, fans can buy official merchandise, visit the museum dedicated to the club's history and participate in exclusive events. It is a place where fans can feel part of the Rossoneri family.

Casa Milan regularly hosts events and meetings with players and club legends. These events are a unique opportunity for fans to meet their idols and experience unforgettable moments. The facility is also used for press conferences and official presentations.

Inside Casa Milan, visitors can enjoy a high-quality restaurant and bistro. Here, you can enjoy traditional Italian dishes in an elegant and cosy ambience. It is the perfect place to relax after a visit to the museum or a special event.

The Inter FC Headquarters

The Inter FC headquarters is located at Viale della Liberazione 16/18, in the modern Porta Nuova district, known for its skyscrapers. This building, called 'The Corner', was designed by Alfonso Femia and occupies five floors, from the sixth to the tenth, with over 200 workstations. Inter moved here in 2019, leaving the historic Corso Vittorio Emanuele II headquarters.

The Inter headquarters has changed location several times over the years. Initially located in Foro Buonaparte, it then moved to Piazza Duse and later to Via Durini. From 2009 to 2019, the headquarters was in Corso Vittorio Emanuele II, near the Duomo, a symbolic location for the club's successes, including the Triplete years.

The current headquarters is located in one of the most dynamic areas of Milan, easily accessible thanks to its proximity to the Garibaldi station and metro lines. This district is chosen by many important companies and offers numerous services, making it an ideal location for managers and players.

The venue regularly hosts events and conferences, although access for fans is limited. However, on special occasions, such as meetings organised with Inter Clubs, fans can visit the offices and attend events.

Despite the limited access, the venue offers various services for fans, including special meetings and organised tours. During the celebrations for the last Scudetto, the managers celebrated with the fans from the terrace, an unforgettable moment for all present.

The Derby della Madonnina

The Derby della Madonnina is one of Milan's most eagerly awaited and heartfelt football events. The name 'derby della madonnina' derives from the statue of Our Lady of the Assumption towering over Milan Cathedral, the symbol of the city. The first official match between AC Milan and Inter Milan was held in 1909 and since then, every encounter has been charged with passion and rivalry.

Over the years, there have been many memorable matches that have marked derby history. Each match is an opportunity for fans to relive historic moments and hope for new victories. The matches between Sandro Mazzola and Gianni Rivera in the 1970s are just a few examples of how this derby has provided unforgettable emotions.

Derby statistics are always a subject of discussion among fans. Who has won the most games? What was the most sensational result? In addition to wins and losses, there are many curiosities linked to this event, such as the nicknames given to the fans of the two teams: Inter supporters were called 'baùscia' while Milan supporters were known as 'casciavìt'. These nicknames have been lost over time and have become rarer.

How to Experience the Derby in Milan

Living the derby in Milan is a unique experience. The city is transformed, the bars and restaurants are filled with fans and the atmosphere is electrifying. Whether you're at the San Siro stadium or a club in the centre, the excitement of the derby can be felt everywhere. Make sure you arrive early to get a good seat and get ready to experience a day of pure football passion.

THE SAN SIRO STADIUM

Opening Hours

The San Siro Stadium is open every day, with opening times varying according to the season. During summer hours, visits are possible from 9:30 a.m. to 6 p.m., while in winter the closing time is earlier at 5 p.m. However, it is important to note that hours may vary in the event of matches or special events.

Prices and Tickets

The cost of a ticket to visit the stadium is around EUR 30 for adults, while children under 15 pay a reduced rate of EUR 25. You can buy tickets online, which is recommended to avoid long queues at the ticket office. With this San Siro stadium ticket, you will have access to a self-guided tour that allows you to explore every corner of the stadium.

Guided and Autonomous Tours

The stadium tour can be taken in both guided and self-guided mode. The guided tour offers a detailed overview of the stadium's history and curiosities, while the self-guided tour allows you to explore at your own pace. Both tours include access to the San Siro Museum, where you can admire memorabilia and trophies from the Milan and Inter teams. The tour also includes access to the dressing rooms, the pitch and the stands, offering a complete and immersive experience.

History of the San Siro Stadium

The San Siro Stadium, built at the behest of Rossoneri president Piero Pirelli, was inaugurated on 19 September 1926 with a friendly match between Inter and Milan. The idea was to create a sports hub next to the existing hippodrome. Initially, the stadium had only four stands and could accommodate 35,000 spectators.

In the 1930s, ownership of the stadium passed to the City of Milan, which started extension works. The capacity was increased to 55,000 spectators. In the 1960s, the famous propeller-shaped ramps were added, increasing the capacity to 80,000 for safety reasons.

The Third Ring and the 1990 World Cup

For the 1990 World Cup, a third ring was added, bringing the stadium to its current form. Although commonly known as San Siro, the stadium is officially named after Giuseppe Meazza, a footballer who played for both Inter and AC Milan and was world champion with the Italian national team.

The San Siro Museum

The San Siro Museum is a must-see for every football fan. Opened in the 1990s, it was the first museum in Italy to open inside a stadium. Here, visitors can immerse themselves in the history of Milan's two teams, Inter and AC Milan, through a vast collection of unique memorabilia.

Inside the museum, you will find historical jerseys, cups, trophies, medals, balls, and shoes that tell the story of the victories and highlights of the two teams. Each item on display has a story to tell, making the visit an exciting and engaging experience.

The Milan Inter vs. United Jersey

One of the most fascinating objects in the museum is the Milan Inter United shirt, a symbol of unity and collaboration between the two rival teams. This jersey represents a unique and rare piece of history that attracts the attention of all visitors.

3 DAYS IN MILAN

If you love art: Leonardo da Vinci's Milan

Leonardo da Vinci arrived in Milan in 1482 and stayed for 18 years. He was about 30 years of age and was seeking his fortune.

We have collected Leonardo da Vinci's places in Milan in this tour. Places where he worked or lived: some require a long visit, others only a few minutes.

The museums and monuments are not just about Leonardo, of course. As with all the other tours, you can go through the stages freely: in the order you want and choosing whether to go on foot or by metro.

Remember one key thing: the visit to the Last Supper must be booked online well in advance. Really. Do it.

Conca dell'Incoronata, also known as 'Conca di Leonardo'.

We are in **Via San Marco, a street in the centre of Milan**. One of the Navigli once passed through here, and Da Vinci worked on a system to connect the Naviglio Martesana, coming from the north, to the city's Navigli circle.

This was no small problem, because the Naviglio Martesana had a different height from the circle. A basin was therefore needed to solve the problem, allowing for smooth navigation.

The solution found was particularly ingenious, with a basin created at the end of the 15th century by Giuliano Guasconi and Bartolomeo della Valle, with the advice of Leonardo, who drew up the first plans as early as 1482.

The Brera Art Gallery

This museum houses two drawings by Leonardo da Vinci and a number of works by his followers, the best known of which are certainly Bernardino Luini and Cesare da Sesto.

The Sforza Castle

The rooms of the Museums housed in the Castle contain some works by Leonardo da Vinci.

The Castle's Sala delle Asse has a vault with a large fresco by Da Vinci. In the Trivulziana Library, also inside the Castle, is the Codice Trivulziano, a collection of drawings and writings on military and religious themes.

In general, the Castello Sforzesco houses several museums and its rooms are worth a closer look.

Piazza della Scala

When you are done, exit and continue to Piazza della Scala, passing by the Duomo and the Galleria Vittorio Emanuele. Here stands the Monument to Leonardo da Vinci, right in the centre of the square.

A few steps away is the Leonardo3 Museum (full admission 12 euros). This is an exhibition, which began as a temporary and then became permanent, of reconstructions of Leonardo's models and works. Interesting to understand the more technical aspects of his genius.

Ambrosian Art Gallery

Access to the Pinacoteca Ambrosiana costs 15 euros, if you have no reductions (we recommend, as you know, the Abbonamento Musei). A complete visit of the museum takes at least an hour, given the large number of works present.

Several paintings were made by Leonardo's disciples. If you want to point straight at him, in the Leonardi Hall there is the Portrait of a Musician, dated 1485. And in the last rooms you will find drawings from the Codex Atlanticus on display in rotation, in a truly impressive setting.

Last Supper (Basilica of Santa Maria delle Grazie)

At the **Basilica of Santa Maria delle Grazie** one of Leonardo's best-known works, which rivals the Mona Lisa, awaits you: the Last Supper, or Cenacolo.

The fresco is located inside an imposing basilica with a graceful interior. But most visitors ignore it, waiting to see the Last Supper.

I would like to remind you for the umpteenth time that booking the visit is compulsory and must be done online. The booking time must be strictly adhered to, by presenting yourself at the ticket office first.

You pass a quick security check and are ushered into the Upper Room, which is located on one of the walls. Don't forget to also take a look at the fresco of the Crucifixion, on the opposite side, which completes the sense of the room's decoration. It is a work by Donato Montorfano, designed specifically to confront the Last Supper: on the one hand, Jesus pledges to offer his material body for the remission of sins, and on the other, he fulfils that pledge by dying on the cross.

You only have 15 minutes in that room, then they will let you out to make room for the next round of visits. Admission to the Cenacolo is not included in the Musei Lombardia season ticket.

Le Vigne di Leonardo

At the exit of the Cenacolo look across the street. There is Casa Atellani, which unfortunately can no longer be visited because it was bought by a private individual to build a hotel. It is a 15th century palace, historically interesting, with a peculiarity. In its garden was a vineyard, given by Ludovico il Moro, Duke of Milan, to our very own Leonardo da Vinci. It was the year 1498 and Leonardo left Milan, which had just been conquered by the French, already the following year. In short, Leonardo's vineyard is little more than a suggestion, but while you are in front of Casa Atellani, try to imagine Leonardo walking between the rows.

Milan Museum of Science and Technology

To whom could a Museum of Science and Technology be dedicated if not to Leonardo da Vinci, who spent such significant years in this city? The museum is suitable for science enthusiasts rather than history buffs, but it also exhibits models based on Leonardo's drawings and some of his designs.

If you love art: discovering Hayez's Kisses

Francesco Hayez, a painter who emblematically represents Italian Romanticism, left the world one of the most famous and recognisable works of the 19th century: 'The Kiss'.

This painting, full of passion and symbolic nuances, captures the essence of an era and continues to fascinate art experts and painting lovers of every generation.

Everyone in Milan knows where Hayez's Kiss is: the most famous version is kept in the last room of the Pinacoteca di Brera.

Not everyone, however, knows that this extraordinary painting is not a one-off, quite the contrary. The Kiss has been painted in several versions. At the Gallerie d'Italia in Milan, in 2016, the three most famous ones were placed side by side, in a historical and hopefully not unrepeatable exhibition.

Let us try to understand more with a virtual tour of Hayez's Kisses (most of the works, however, you can go and see for yourself).

Brera Art Gallery

At the Brera is Hayez's first Kiss, the one that started all this fuss about lips being full of passion. The full title of the work was 'The Kiss. Episode of Youth. Costumes of the 14th century'. It arrived in the Pinacoteca di Brera a few decades later.

The picture was painted in 1859, a key period in the Italian unification process, infused with patriotic fervour and a desire for independence.

Francesco Hayez was best known for portraits and historical scenes, yet he painted a passionate couple exchanging a kiss in the shadow of a secret passageway, a symbol of clandestine relationships but also of the conspiracies of the time.

The man, wrapped in a red cloak that could symbolise passion or the revolutionary cause, gently holds the woman, dressed in harmonious shades of blue and ivory that suggest purity and devotion.

The figures are immersed in a dark environment, as if to signify that their passion shines brightly in a time of uncertainty. The chequered floor may symbolise the complex political game of the Italian Risorgimento.

The meaning of Hayez's kiss, at least according to this common reading, also explains its success: the Second War of Independence had just ended and in that painting some people saw the farewell kiss of the hero volunteer leaving for the front and bidding farewell to his beloved. Not knowing whether he will return.

It must be said, then, that the kiss is in itself a key theme in art, the representation of a spontaneous gesture of affection, love, desire and physical passion. A few decades later, for example, it was also chosen by Klimt for one of his most famous paintings.

Here, this work was a resounding success. Huge. Hayez was inundated with requests for replicas and new versions. To which the painter was happy to give a positive response, enjoying the success and the takings. This was not, by the way, a unique case in his career: it also happened to him on other occasions to produce replicas, well paid, of his successful paintings.

This is why we know, with certainty, that there are other versions of Hayez's Kiss.

Number two is the Mylius version dated 1861, commissioned by entrepreneur Federico Mylius and now part of a private collection. It stands out because the girl is wearing a white dress: there is a certain reference to the Italian flag, as the boy is wearing a green cape and red tights instead. It may be that Hayez wanted to ride the 'Risorgimento' interpretation of his own work, or that there was a specific request from the commissioner.

Version three fetched $1.865 million at a Christie's auction in 2016. It was painted in 1867 for the Paris Expo and adds a veil thrown over the steps and a half column behind the protagonists to the scene, plus it moves the mullioned window in the background. Hayez kept it until his death, then it even ended up in the family of the Tsar of Russia.

Version four is the Kiss entrusted by the painter to Adele Appiani (one of his mistresses), the traces of which have been lost.

The fifth version would be dated 1859 and is characterised by its small size, 55 x 40 cm. A catalogue of Hayez's works, dated 1994, attributes it to Carolina Zucchi, who was also a lover of the indefatigable painter, and assumes that it is still with her heirs even after more than 160 years.

At Villa Carlotta on Lake Como, another Hayez painting centred on the theme of the kiss can be seen. The title of the painting is 'Romeo and Juliet's Last Kiss' and it is a particularly interesting work because it is dated 1823: 36 years before the kiss that was an overwhelming success. Yet in many aspects, starting with the pose, it is already reminiscent of later kisses.

Are we done? Absolutely not. Because then there are the watercolour versions of Hayez's kiss. One, dated 1859, is on display at the Pinacoteca Ambrosiana in Milan. But since Hayez, faced with the great success of his work, made several copies, it is possible that there are other replicas and exemplars of the watercolour versions as well.

And it is quite possible that more of these watercolours exist, who knows where.

The other kisses of Brera

In the same Pinacoteca di Brera we also find two other kisses linked to Hayez's work.

One is Gerolamo Induno's 'Triste Presentimento'. If you look closely at this painting, behind the girl who is the protagonist of the painting and next to the bust of Garibaldi, there is a small painting of Francesco Hayez's kiss. A homage that Gerolamo Induno pays to Francesco Hayez and his most famous work.

Another kiss can be found outside the Brera Palace: looking at the Palace, in the small square on the right, since 1890 there has been a memorial dedicated to Francesco Hayez, who was one of the teachers at the Brera Academy for years. The work was created by

Francesco Barzaghi and on the left side, engraved in bronze, is the master's famous 'Kiss'.

The tip: save money with tourist passes

Tourist pass cards are a useful and very convenient service that can be found in all major cities around the world. As far as tourist passes in Milan are concerned, we recommend three:

- **Yes Milano Pass:** includes transport and admission to various attractions;
- **Milano Museo Card:** annual pass to enter many public museums at a flat rate of 15 euros;
- **Abbonamento Musei Lombardia:** valid for one year, it allows access to dozens of monuments, museums and attractions in Milan and the Lombardy Region.

These cards can be purchased online and are useful for those who want to plan their trip in advance, organising the things to see and optimising their time and costs.

They are cards designed for tourists, but they are also useful for those who live in Milan or in the province, and want to experience their city differently: it happens very often that we do not know the cultural heritage that our city offers us, and that is really a shame.

The purchase of pass cards is personal: they are neither transferable nor assignable. Identity and document checks at the ticket office are very frequent.

Yes Milano City Pass

Yes Milano City Pass is a pay-as-you-go app that allows you to use public transport, enter some attractions for free and get discounts for three days.

The app must first be downloaded and then activated: the Pass is valid after activation, not after downloading.

There are two versions:

- Standard, 60 euros: includes public transport, Duomo with Terrace, Castello Sforzesco, Museo del Novecento, a 'Premium' activity of your choice from a catalogue, other minor museums and conventions for some museums and activities;
- All Inclusive, 90 euro: includes everything in Standard plus the La Scala Theatre Museum, the National Museum of Science and Technology, the Triennale Design Museum, the Pinacoteca Ambrosiana, the Crypt of San Sepolcro and other museums.

The Yes Milano Card is useful if you want to spend a lot of time visiting museums and monuments. It costs less than the sum of all entrance fees and public transport tickets, but you have to consider which museums you really want to visit.

Remember that admission is often free on the first Sunday of the month. And that some museums offer reduced tickets for students under 25, minors, seniors over 65, journalists (including European ones, provided they have an ID card) and other categories.

MILAN MUSEUM CARD

It lasts one year, costs 15 euros and allows you to enter the Civic Museums of the Municipality of Milan for one year. It also includes a 20% discount on tickets for temporary exhibitions at Palazzo Reale, PAC Padiglione d'Arte Contemporanea and Fabbrica del Vapore.

It is valid in the Castello Sforzesco Museums - Picture Gallery, Pietà Rondanini Museum, Museum of Decorative Arts, Museum of Furniture and Wooden Sculptures, Museum of Prehistory and Protohistory, Museum of Ancient Art, Museum of Musical Instruments; Museum of the 20th Century; GAM | Gallery of Modern Art; Museum of Natural History; Archaeological Museum; Civic Aquarium.

If there are temporary exhibitions with a surcharge, you only have to pay the difference to the regular ticket.

You can buy it on Vivaticket in digital format (no need to print it out) or at the ticket offices of the Galleria d'Arte Moderna, Museo Archeologico, Museo del Novecento, Castello Sforzesco Museums, Acquario Civico, Museo di Storia Naturale.

Tourist Museum Card

An open-access season ticket that offers free entry for 3 consecutive days to all Milan's Civic Museums (one entry in each museum). It costs 12 euros.

It is valid in the Castello Sforzesco Museums - Picture Gallery, Pietà Rondanini Museum, Museum of Decorative Arts, Museum of Furniture and Wooden Sculptures, Museum of Prehistory and Protohistory, Museum of Ancient Art, Museum of Musical Instruments; Museum of the 20th Century; GAM | Gallery of Modern Art; Museum of Natural History; Archaeological Museum; Civic Aquarium.

If there are temporary exhibitions with a surcharge, you only have to pay the difference to the regular ticket.

You can buy it on Vivaticket in digital format (no need to print it out) or at the ticket offices of the Galleria d'Arte Moderna, Museo Archeologico, Museo del Novecento, Castello Sforzesco Museums, Acquario Civico, Museo di Storia Naturale.

The card is valid from the day the first entry is made, regardless of the date of purchase. It is not nominative.

THE LOMBARDIA MUSEI SUBSCRIPTION

The Lombardia Musei is a crazy card. For only 45 euro it allows you to enter over 120 museums in Milan and its region: it is valid for one year.

A promotion that started in Lombardy and expanded to Piedmont and Valle d'Aosta.

It allows everyone to explore the artistic and cultural heritage of these regions. It includes admission to museums and places of historical interest such as archaeological sites, monasteries, convents, museums of ancient, modern and contemporary art, royal residences, as well as villas, gardens, castles and botanical gardens - wonderful places that people often don't know about even though they live near them.

The Lombardy Museums season ticket covers the entire region, the sites and activities included in the package can be found in Milan, Bergamo, Brescia, Como, Cremona, Lecco, Lodi, Mantua, Monza and Brianza, Pavia, Sondrio and Varese, and are divided both by location and date, making it even easier to organise yourself.

In Milan, the Abbonamento Lombardia Musei circuit includes the Duomo Museum, the Museo del Novecento, the Archaeological Museum, the Gallerie d'Italia, the Triennale, the Museo Nazionale della Scienza e della Tecnologia Leonardo da Vinci and the Museo Diocesano, as well as the Acquario Civico, the Museo di Storia Naturale, the Castello Sforzesco, the park of the Anfiteatro Romano, the Casa Museo Boschi di Stefano, the Studio Francesco Messina, the Museo Poldi Pezzoli, the Hangar Bicocca and many other spaces.

For families with children there is the MUBA Children's Museum, the Interactive Museum of Cinema and the Bergamo Gallery of Modern and Contemporary Art.

For those who love villas and open-air excursions, the season ticket includes admission to the Villa Reale in Monza and Villa della Porta Bozzolo in Casalzuigno in the province of Varese, Villa Carlotta in Tremezzo in the province of Como, and the 'Lorenzo Rota' Botanical Garden in Bergamo, where you can admire rare and beautiful species.

Where to buy it

The subscription can be purchased online, via the official e-commerce, or at the ticket offices of the most important museums.

On the website you will find a complete map with all sales outlets divided by province, with addresses, opening hours and useful directions.

How much does it cost

The Lombardia Musei season ticket costs 52 euro, but there are various interesting conventions. Those over 65 can get the Senior season ticket for 42 euro, young people between the ages of 15 and 26 can purchase the Young version for 30 euro, and children up to 14 years of age for only 20 euro.

The Region of Lombardy rewards those who already have other subscriptions to theatres or associations with a 5 euro discount, you can see the complete list on the website.

The Lombardy Museums card also includes several attractions in Valle d'Aosta.

There is also Abbonamento Musei Extra, also valid for one year, which also includes dozens of attractions in Piedmont: the formula for three regions (Lombardy, Piedmont and Valle d'Aosta) costs 87 euro, discounted to 80 euro for the over 65s, 62 euro for young people between 15 and 26 years of age, and 40 euro for those under 14.

Beyond Milan: 1-day Trips

Lake Como

Getting to Lake Como from Milan is quite simple: you can go by car or one of the local trains. With its breathtaking views and sparkling waters, this lake is world famous.

One of the most popular activities is a scenic cruise on the lake. During the cruise, you will have the opportunity to admire the beautiful villas and gardens that line the shores. Don't forget to stop at Bellagio, known as the 'Pearl of Lake Como'. Here, you can stroll through the picturesque streets and enjoy spectacular views of the Alps.

If you prefer adventure, Lake Como is surrounded by mountains that offer numerous hikes. You can climb Mount Grona or Mount San Primo for unforgettable panoramic views. In addition, the Sentiero del Viandante (Wayfarer's Path) allows you to explore ancient paths through villages and forests, with spectacular views of the lake.

For those who love history and culture, Como offers historical monuments, a charming old town and the Duomo di Como. Don't miss the opportunity to visit the Tempio Voltiano, dedicated to the inventor of the electric battery, Alessandro Volta.

Venice

Visiting Venice from Milan is feasible: Italo and Frecciarossa fast trains take visitors directly to the gates of the city, just cross the first canal and enter Venice!

It is one of the most romantic cities in the world and a must for anyone visiting Italy. Its lagoons, cobbled streets and unique architecture make it a place like no other. On a day trip to Venice from Milan, you can explore the city with a local guide and learn about its history and beautiful attractions.

Don't miss the Rialto Bridge, St Mark's Square and the Bridge of Sighs. Take a gondola ride through the lagoons, a typical and unforgettable experience. If you visit during Carnival, you will be lucky enough to experience one of the most famous Carnivals in the world. If you have time, it is worth visiting Murano, famous for its glass-blowing traditions.

VERONA

Verona is the famous city of the Arena and Romeo and Juliet. To go to Verona from Milan we recommend a train journey of about 1 hour and 15 minutes (with the faster Italo and Frecciarossa trains). The centre of Verona is very interesting and can be explored on foot, directly from the train station. From Milan it is also possible to reach Verona by car, although the traffic on the A4 motorway is always quite heavy.

Several agencies offer organised one-day tours from Milan to Verona.

MONZA

A trip from Milan to Monza is an excellent choice. This Brianza city has a fascinating history, although less well known than other Italian cities. Strolling through the historical centre, you can discover the Duomo, where the treasure of the Longobard queen Teodolinda is kept.

The Villa Reale in Monza is another must-see. This beautiful building often hosts interesting exhibitions and its huge park is ideal for a stroll or a bike ride. If you are travelling with children, the park offers plenty of space to play and relax.

The city is particularly suitable for bicycle lovers. Monza is perfect for exploring on two wheels, allowing you to fully enjoy its natural and architectural beauty.

TURIN

Turin, once the first capital of Italy, is an easy destination for a day trip from Milan. Fast Italo and Frecciarossa trains connect it to the Milan Central and Milan Porta Garibaldi stations in about 1 hour. We recommend the train because it takes you right into the centre of Turin.

This elegant city, renovated for the Olympic Games, offers many architectural gems such as the Royal Palace, Palazzo Madama and the Mole Antonelliana. Turin also boasts a large number of historic cafés with an ancient atmosphere and the world's most important Egyptian Museum outside Egypt. In addition, it is the Italian capital of chocolate and is famous for its good food.

LAKE MAGGIORE

Just over an hour's drive from Milan, Lake Maggiore welcomes you with its timeless beauty. This lake, the second largest in Italy, is perfect for a day trip. It can be reached by train and car, but the best thing is to get off at one of the resorts and explore it using the local boat lines.

You can explore the city centre and then set off on a boat tour around the lake, stopping at the charming Borromean Islands. The islands, with their gardens and historic villas, will make you feel as if you have stepped back in time.

Lake Maggiore is surrounded by hills that protect it from northern winds, creating a mild and pleasant climate. Its shores extend between Lombardy, Piedmont and Switzerland, offering a variety of breathtaking landscapes. Among the natural and artistic beauties not to be missed are the botanical gardens, parks and nature reserves.

Don't forget to visit Stresa, one of the most famous resorts on the lake. If you love nature, the gardens of Villa Taranto will leave you speechless.

There is also a train + boat formula to explore some of the most beautiful corners of the area.

CINQUE TERRE

The Cinque Terre are one of the most fascinating destinations you can visit on a day trip from Milan. This coastal area is famous for its picturesque, colourful villages and crystal-clear waters.

You can easily reach Monterosso by train from Milano Centrale in about 2 hours and 55 minutes. If you prefer travelling by car, take the A7 motorway and then the A12, following the signs for Carrodano/Levanto and finally for Monterosso a Mare. This is a demanding excursion, so we recommend spending at least one night in the Cinque Terre.

If you are short of time, you can take a boat trip to admire the coast from the sea. If you have more time, you can walk the Sentiero Azzurro, a 12-kilometre route that connects all the villages of the Cinque Terre, offering breathtaking views.

A romantic experience is the Via dell'Amore, a short path connecting Riomaggiore and Manarola.

Day tours to the Cinque Terre from Milan cost about €130 and last about 13 hours. If you want pickup from your hotel, you can pay an extra €10-€20. The Cinque Terre is a must-visit destination for those who love nature, the sea and picture-postcard landscapes.

Mantua

Mantua, also known as 'Italy's Sleeping Beauty', is a lakeside city located in the heart of the Po Valley. This city offers a quiet and relaxing atmosphere, far from the tourist crowds of more famous destinations. Visit the Palazzo Ducale, the former residence of the Duke of Mantua, and be fascinated by its history. Don't miss the Palazzo Te, a Renaissance masterpiece, and the Rotonda di San Lorenzo, one of the city's oldest churches. If you have time, take a walk along the three lakes formed by the Mincio River that surround Mantua.

Bergamo Alta

You may know Bergamo for its Orio al Serio airport, where Ryanair and many other airlines, not only low-cost, land. Bergamo is a modern, industrial city, but it retains a perfectly preserved and very interesting old historical centre to explore, called Bergamo Alta. To organise your day trip to Bergamo, you need to arrive in the city by train or car. And then go up to the Upper Town on foot or by the unmissable funicular railway.

Don't forget to explore the upper city and have lunch in one of the excellent restaurants in the old town.

Vigevano

For a trip from Milan by train or car, one of the most interesting destinations is certainly Vigevano. This town in the Lomellina region is a little artistic jewel just waiting to be discovered. Its Piazza Ducale is one of the most beautiful in Italy, with the elegance of its arcades, the peculiar concave façade of its cathedral and the oddity of the many chimneys - all different from each other - on the roofs of the buildings.

Palazzo Ducale, the Leonardiana exhibition and the Shoe Museum are worth a visit. And if you can arrange public transport, travel as far as Morimondo Abbey to admire one of the masterpieces of Cistercian architecture.

Pavia

Pavia is a perfect destination for a day trip from Milan. The city offers a quiet and charming atmosphere. Strolling through the streets of the centre, you can discover monuments such as the Duomo, the churches of San Michele Maggiore and San Pietro in Ciel d'Oro. Don't forget to visit the 'salotto buono' of Piazza della Vittoria.

A word of advice: don't miss the Castello Visconteo with its Civic Museums! Afterwards, take a walk to the Ponte Coperto and cross it to reach the characteristic houses of Borgo Ticino.

If you still have time, take the train and visit the Certosa di Pavia, one of the most important monastic complexes in Italy.

Special Occasions in Milan

Christmas and New Year in Milan

Milan is a city famous for fashion and design. It is therefore a great place for Christmas shopping (and remember that sales and special offers start in early January).

From mid-November, the streets of the city centre begin to be decorated with Christmas-themed light installations. Many large Christmas trees also appear in the centre. The most famous is the one in Piazza del Duomo, often the subject of discussion and controversy.

Other Christmas trees decorate the main city centre squares and are frequently linked to corporate sponsorships or specific charity initiatives.

Also, not to be missed are the Christmas decorations in the Galleria Vittorio Emanuele II: if you arrive at the centre when it is already dark, remember to look up.

Christmas Markets

In December, the heart of Milan is transformed into a magical Christmas village with the Christmas Market in Piazza Duomo. This event is one of the most eagerly awaited and loved Christmas events by the Milanese and tourists alike. The characteristic little wooden houses offer a wide range of products, from traditional foods to Christmas decorations and souvenirs such as boule à neige. The entire perimeter of the cathedral is enlivened by countless stalls that make the atmosphere even more atmospheric.

THE OH BEJ! OH BEJ!

The Oh Bej! Oh Bej! Fair is one of Milan's oldest and best-loved Christmas events. Its origins date back to 1288, when the city's patron saint, Sant'Ambrogio, was celebrated. The fair takes place every year from 7 to 10 December, coinciding with the feast of Sant'Ambrogio, and attracts thousands of visitors. The name of the fair derives from the Milanese exclamation 'Oh bej! Oh bej!', meaning 'Oh belli! Oh belli!', and is said to have originated in 1510, when Giannetto Castiglione, a papal envoy, distributed sweets and toys to Milanese children.

At the Oh Bej! Oh Bej! Fair you will find a wide range of products, from traditional toys and antiques to clothes, Christmas decorations and typical sweets. It is the perfect place to find unique gifts and immerse yourself in the Milanese Christmas atmosphere. There is no shortage of winter delicacies such as smoked chestnuts and castagnaccio, which will make you feel the true spirit of Christmas.

During the fair, in addition to shopping, you can participate in numerous special events. There are live shows, musical performances and activities for children. The fair takes place in the beautiful setting of the Castello Sforzesco, making the experience even more magical.

Admission is free, so you have no excuse not to drop by and experience the magic of Christmas in Milan.

Handicrafts at the Milan Rho-Pero Trade Fair

Artigianato in Fiera is an unmissable event for those who love handmade products. With over 3,000 stands of craftsmen from all over the world, you can find unique and original objects. This fair is a real journey between cultures, where each stand tells a different story. Don't miss the opportunity to discover unique and quality pieces.

The fair is generally open every day from 10:00 to 22:30, but you should check the updated schedule for each edition. It is a perfect opportunity to do your Christmas shopping and find special gifts for your loved ones. Remember that admission is free, but registration on the official website is required.

The fair takes place in Rho, just 20 minutes from the centre of Milan. You can reach it easily by public transport or by car. The Fieramilano exhibition centre offers a full range of services for visitors, making your experience even more enjoyable. There is no excuse not to attend this extraordinary event!

Milan Fashion Week

Milan Fashion Week 2025 is one of the most anticipated events in the fashion world. Here are the dates for 2025:

- 17-21 January 2025, Men's Fashion Week (autumn/winter 2025/26)
- 25 February to 3 March 2025, Women's Fashion Week (Autumn/Winter 2025/26)
- 20 to 24 June, Fashion Week Men (Spring/Summer 2026)

- 23-29 September, Women's Fashion Week (Spring/Summer 2026)

Milan Fashion Week is not just fashion shows, but a complete experience involving the whole city. During this week, Milan is transformed into a stage for unique and unmissable events. Here's what you can't miss.

USEFUL TIPS FOR THOSE VISITING MILAN DURING FASHION WEEK

Where to stay

If you are coming to Milan for Fashion Week, book your hotel now! The best accommodations sell out fast. Consider San Babila, one of the city's most elegant districts. This allows you to be close to the main events and have a star experience.

Getting around the city

Getting around Milan during Fashion Week can be complicated due to traffic and roads closed for events. The best way to get around is to use public transport or walk. The city is well served by trams, buses and metro, which allows you to easily reach all the event locations. In addition, strolling through the streets of the city centre will give you the opportunity to discover hidden corners and admire luxury shop windows.

Events open to the public

Although fashion shows are often reserved for fashion insiders, there are events open to the public that allows you to experience the unique atmosphere of Milan Fashion Week. For instance, you can participate in exhibitions, art installations and collection presentations at various locations around the city. Don't forget to visit the Fashion Quadrilateral, a 'Arabian Nights' place where luxury and elegance are at home.

Tour of iconic fashion locations

Milan is full of iconic fashion-related places you can visit. Stroll down Via Montenapoleone, Via della Spiga and Corso Venezia to admire the shop windows of high-fashion shops. Don't miss the Galleria Vittorio Emanuele II, a true temple of shopping with its breathtaking architecture. Even if you are not an insider, you will breathe the air of fashion in every corner of the city.

The History of Milan Fashion Week

The first official edition of Milan Fashion Week was held in 1975, consolidating the city's role as the epicentre of fashion in Italy. However, the roots of this event go back to the 1950s, when G.B. Giorgini presented Italian haute couture collections to foreign journalists and buyers in Florence. This event marked the beginning of the international recognition of Italian fashion.

In the 1970s, Milan became the capital of Italian fashion, hosting the first prêt-à-porter shows at the Fiera di Milano. Here, big names such as Walter Albini, Krizia and Missoni began to make a name for themselves. Over the years, Milan Fashion Week has grown to become one of the most anticipated events in the fashion world.

Milan Fashion Week has seen historic moments and memorable fashion shows that have left their mark. From the first catwalks of Giorgio Armani and Versace to recent innovations and collaborations, each edition brings with it a mix of tradition and novelty that continues to amaze and fascinate the public.

THE SALONE DEL MOBILE AND DESIGN WEEK

8 - 13 April 2025

The week of the Salone del Mobile is particularly intense for Milan. Hundreds of events are organised all over the city, public transport is full, traffic is hellish, restaurants are super-booked, hotel and flat prices shoot up. But Milan is still almost always sold out and finding a place to sleep or eat becomes a feat.

Here are our tips for preparing for the Salone del Mobile 2025, scheduled from 8 to 13 April 2025, in conjunction with Design Week 2025.

TIPS FOR VISITING MILAN DURING THE SALONE DEL MOBILE

Book early: cheap rooms are few and far between

To enjoy Milan Design Week to the fullest, it is essential to book accommodation well in advance. If you wait too long, finding nice accommodation at reasonable prices becomes a mission impossible. The ideal is to book as early as February to avoid surprises and to guarantee you a comfortable place close to the main events.

Stress-free travel planning

Getting around Milan during Design Week can be tricky, so it's best to plan your trip in advance. Forget the private car: traffic is a nightmare and parking spaces are scarce.

Opt instead for the train or plane and take advantage of the city's public transport, which works very well. Metro, trams and buses will take you wherever you want to go without stress.

Subscribe to the Fuorisalone Newsletter

A trick that few people know is to subscribe to the Fuorisalone newsletter. This allows you to receive updates on the most interesting events and installations. Many of the coolest things to see in Milan during Design Week are communicated via the newsletter. Don't forget to also follow the Fuorisalone on Instagram for previews and trivia.

The Unmissable Districts of the Fuorisalone

During Milan Design Week, there are some districts that you absolutely cannot miss. Each area has its own unique character and offers different and fascinating experiences.

Brera is the historical heart of design in Milan. Here you will find the most iconic and high-end companies such as Flos, Versace and Natuzzi.

Tortona is the district where it all began. Here, design is more alternative and experimental. You will find exhibition installations both outdoors and in closed spaces, such as Opificio 31. The area is famous for events such as Tortona Rocks and the Superdesign Show. Every year, this neighbourhood is transformed into a veritable laboratory of creativity.

Getting Around Milan During Design Week

Getting around Milan during Design Week may seem complicated, but with a few tips it becomes child's play. Milan Design Week is an event that attracts thousands of visitors, so it is important to know how to get around without stress.

Using public transport

Public transport is the best choice for getting around the city. The metro, trams, and buses cover all the main areas and allow you to easily reach the various events. Remember that to go to the Fair, you will need a special ticket.

Renting scooters and bicycles

If you prefer a more environmentally friendly and fun option, you can rent scooters and bicycles. There are many rental stations scattered around the city, allowing you to move quickly between events. Just be careful not to park them wildly!

Avoiding the private car

Using a private car during Design Week is not a good idea. Traffic can be heavy and finding parking is almost impossible. Better to rely on public transport or rental options to enjoy the event without stress.

PRACTICAL TIPS FOR A PERFECT VISIT

Wear comfortable shoes

During Milan Design Week, you will be walking a lot. Wearing comfortable shoes is essential to enjoy every moment without suffering. Don't underestimate this advice, because the distances between events can be considerable.

Bringing a bag

Between brochures, catalogues and small gadgets, you will accumulate a lot of material. Take a light and roomy shopping bag with you to collect everything without hassle. This allows you to keep your hands free and move more nimbly between events.

Planning visits by neighbourhood

Milan Design Week is a sea of opportunities, with some 1300 events scattered throughout the city. To avoid wasting time and energy, plan your visits by neighbourhood. Devote a day to Brera, another to Tortona and so on. This will help you optimise your movements and enjoy each district to the full.

How to avoid crowds

To best enjoy the Salone del Mobile without stress, we recommend visiting the pavilions on weekdays and arriving early in the morning. Use public transport to get to Fiera Milano Rho and download the official app to stay updated on events and timetables. Remember, the Salone is vast and requires at least a full day to explore thoroughly. Keep a quick pace to avoid missing the most important things!

One last favour

If you liked this guide, please leave a positive review on Amazon. We read all the opinions personally in order to make the product even better.

Look for us on 'My Orders' and leave us a good score, as well as your suggestions!

Thank you.

Printed in Dunstable, United Kingdom